Malone University:
A Commemorative History, 1892–2017

by Jacalynn J. Stuckey

BARCLAY PRESS
Newberg, OR 97132

Malone University:
A Commemorative History, 1892–2017

©2018 by Jacalynn J. Stuckey,

Barclay Press, Inc.
Newberg, Oregon
www.barclaypress.com

Printed in the United States of America.

ISBN 978-1-59498-049-7

Nicholas, Jenaye, and Lena

Contents

Introduction

The weather on March 17, 1892, was fair, but chilly—typical for mid-March in Cleveland, Ohio. It was St. Patrick's Day and Clevelanders were observing the Irish holiday in a variety of ways. Scheduled events included a lecture on "Ireland's Schools and Scholars," a special concert and theater production at a local church, and a banquet sponsored by the Philo Celtic Club. Others patronized local shops and markets. Crow & Whitmarsh was selling men's socks at 25¢ for three pairs and Copco Soap for 4¢ a cake. Fuldheim's was holding a closeout fire sale featuring "$85,000 worth of the finest shoes and boots." Baseball enthusiasts were at League Park to watch the hometown professional team, the Cleveland Spiders, play its first game of the year. *The Plain Dealer* predicted that the 1892 season would be the Spiders' best ever, and it was. That game set the team on course to its winningest season during its brief history, thanks to the talents of the Spiders' soon-to-be-famous pitcher, Denton True "Cy" Young.

Missing from the pages of Cleveland's two main newspapers was any announcement about a new Christian Workers' Training School that was set to launch on St. Patrick's Day. Of course, a tiny institution that drew a mere handful of students on its first day may have seemed too inauspicious to

garner local media attention. Indeed, the unpretentious training school opened with little fanfare and dim prospects. And yet, a century and a quarter later, the school endures—in a new location, with a new name, and with an expanded mission.

The tapestry that is the Malone University story is woven from colorful threads spun long before, but also after, 1892. It starts with J. Walter and Emma Brown Malone but also with the rise of industrial cities, the emergence of urban Bible institutes, and a small denomination of Christians known as Friends. While a full measure of the history of Malone University is not possible in this slim commemorative volume, a brief exploration of the warp and woof of its spiritual foundation offers insights about its long-standing mission and core values.

The story begins with Emma and Walter Malone, founders of what is now Malone University and members of an evangelical branch of the Friends Church. Many of Malone University's 20th and 21st-Century students tended to be unfamiliar

with the Friends before they arrived on campus as freshmen or transfers, even if they were acquainted with the term "Quaker." The Society of Friends was founded in the mid-1600s in the Midlands of England by a group of Christian seekers, most

notably George Fox. Also known as "Quakers" for their tendency to tremble in the Spirit while speaking or praying, Friends began to coalesce during a particularly turbulent time. England was in the midst of a political crisis that led to the temporary dissolution of the monarchy and contributed to concurrent spiritual tensions within the Anglican Church.[1†]

George Fox, born in Leicestershire in 1624, was a deeply spiritual young man who was profoundly affected by the pervasive religious turmoil churning throughout England in the 1640s. He eventually embarked on a spiritual quest until a divine encounter changed the course of his life. As he later recounted in his journal, "Then, oh, then, I heard a voice which said, 'There is one, even Christ Jesus, that can speak to thy condition,' and when I heard it my heart did leap for joy." In this moment, Fox came to believe that it was only through Christ directly and by his grace, not via external rituals or creeds, that one could attain spiritual salvation and perfection.

Drawing from John 15:14–15 as a model for Christian identity, Fox and other like-minded seekers founded what came to be known as the Religious Society of Friends.[2†] Friends emphasized the "Light" of Christ residing inwardly and adopted spiritual practices that reflected the centrality of the Inward Light guiding and directing their lives. Quakers were intentional about their worship, condemned the compartmentalization of one's faith, and endeavored to live holistically. Thus, Friends lived and worshiped simply, met in plain meeting houses rather than ornamented church buildings, and disdained paid pastorates. Rather, they believed the Holy Spirit might lead any one of them to speak during worship. Their clothing was muted in color and style, their homes unadorned. The ordinariness of life was shaped by the Quaker testimonies of simplicity, peace, integrity, community, equality, and stewardship. Friends tended to congregate in fairly homogeneous towns and villages, but they also cared for the poor and disabled, spoke out against injustice, and championed equality for all, regardless of a person's socio-economic class, gender, or ethnicity.

While some Friends diverged from each other on their respective beliefs and practices and separated into different branches over time, Walter and Emma Malone adhered to the fundamental teachings of George Fox, embraced the basic

Quaker testimonies, and endeavored to follow God's command to "do justice, and to love kindness, and to walk humbly with your God" (Micah 6:8). Their school reflected those shared ideals.

The 1922–23 annual catalog recounted the original intent of the Malones: "It has now been thirty years since the word of the Lord came to J. Walter and Emma B. Malone, two young ministers of the Friends Church, calling upon them to open a school for the study of the English Bible, and the training of young people who felt a call to service in the vineyard of the Lord. It was to be a school of co-education in a double sense—co-education in the sense of its being for both young men and women, for they believed in women's ministry; and co-education in the sense of combining Bible study and practical soul-winning work.... As a result, a strong body of Christian workers has gone from the Institution to all parts of the home land and to many foreign fields. The Gospel has been preached by them in clearness and power, and hundreds have been, through their labors, brought to Christ."

This commemorative book charts the 125-year journey of Malone University, from its days as a training school, to a Bible institute, a Bible college, a Christian liberal arts college, and its present standing as a Christian university for the arts, sciences, and professions. It follows the journey of the institution from its beginnings in a small rented house, through moves to two campus locations in Cleveland, Ohio, and, finally, to its current home in Canton, Ohio. It traces the collective history of the school's students, faculty, administrators,

alumni, and friends, from the six adventurous souls who first enrolled on that brisk March day in 1892 to the two thousand who presently attend Malone University.

Alas, it was not possible to include all the names of those who contributed significantly to the founding and growth of Malone University, in ways large and small, over the course of its 125-year history. They are legion. However, even though too many names are absent from these pages, the lack of an acknowledgment should not diminish the importance of their involvement in and support of Emma and Walter's school.

Each chapter that follows explores a specific era in Malone University's history. Of course, it is a challenge to organize any historical account wisely and effectively, and such was the case here.

Two of the risks in dividing the narrative into meaningful, if at times seemingly disparate, chunks are losing sight of both the overarching story and the consequential connections between past and present. However, Malone University underwent a series of significant transitions, transformations, and title changes between 1892 and 2017, so recounting the school's history in chapter form helps to clarify the storyline. Each chapter corresponds with nearly every appellation attached to Walter and Emma's school and, more importantly, to the expanding functions that each new christening embodied. Chapter 1 explores the background and founding of the Malones' Christian training school. Chapter 2 recounts the process by which Walter and Emma's school was chartered by the State of Ohio, entered into a partnership with Cleveland First Friends Church, and expanded its curriculum as a Bible institute. Chapter 3 charts the move from a Bible institute to an accredited four-year Bible College, the move to the Euclid Avenue campus, and the introduction of a junior college

component. Chapter 4 examines Malone's transition from a Bible college to a liberal arts college, the move to Canton, and the efforts to accommodate a more theologically diverse student body. Not surprisingly, given the extraordinary changes during the fifty-two-year Malone College era, this is the longest chapter in the book. Given its length, it is the only chapter divided into sections. Most sections correspond loosely with the administrations of the seven presidents who served during the college era. The final chapter traces the first decade of what is now Malone University, the quasquicentennial celebrations, and a hopeful look toward the future.

The Malone story is interfused with triumphs and disappointments, joys and sorrows, times of celebration and times of testing. Yet, the missional focus on providing "students with an education based on biblical faith in order to develop men and women in intellectual maturity, wisdom, and Christian faith who are committed to serving the church, community, and world" remained the same. As it does now and surely will in years to come.

Chapter 1: The Training School (1892–1899)

Christian Workers Training School and Cleveland Bible Training School

The Malone University story begins in a "prayer closet." Actually, two prayer closets. J. Walter and Emma B. Malone, founders of the first version of what is now Malone University, spent considerable time in prayer together and solitarily in their own inner sanctums. Whether in praise or supplication, Emma and Walter daily found reason to heed Paul's admonition to "pray without ceasing" (I Thessalonians 5:17). So, it is not surprising that Walter and Emma were yet again ensconced in their places of prayer in December 1891. They were seeking divine guidance as they considered launching a rather audacious new venture for two people who had never in their lives attended a college or university. They were praying about a Bible institute.

Of course, there's more to the founding narrative than two prayer closets. Even so, Walter and Emma Malone and their abiding faith are central to the tale. As Malone College President Byron L. Osborne once observed, the Malone University story begins with the "dream of two Quaker young people."

J. Walter Malone was born in 1857 to John Carl and Mary Ann Pennington Malone near the tiny village of Marathon in southwest Ohio. The elder Malones were pious Friends, also known as Quakers, with family roots in Pennsylvania and northeast Ohio. Walter was the seventh of eight children and one of seven sons. Although both parents served as spiritual role models for Walter, he was especially influenced by his mother. Mary Ann was deeply devout, a recorded Friends minister,

and superintendent of a Scripture school at her local Quaker meeting. Walter, who was lightheartedly called "preacher boy" by some of his family members, later recounted in his autobiography, "I hungered to be a preacher like my mother was."

In 1874, Walter spent a semester at Earlham Preparatory School in Richmond, Indiana, and continued his studies at Chickering Institute, a prestigious private academy in Cincinnati, from where he graduated in 1877. Although many of his classmates went on to study at Ivy League universities, Walter did not pursue a baccalaureate degree. Instead, he remained in Cincinnati where he was employed as bookkeeper at a firm owned by the father of a Chickering classmate.

In 1880, two of Walter's brothers invited him to Cleveland. Several of the Malone brothers had become prosperous businessmen in the city. Hezekiah Pennington "HP" Malone, the eldest, was the first to move to Cleveland. HP eventually became co-owner of a successful furniture business with his father-in-law and was wealthy enough to

present his mother ten thousand dollars in cash, a huge sum of money in 1865, to purchase a 109-acre farm. Levi "Harry" Harrison Malone began his lucrative career in Cincinnati before moving to Cleveland, where he operated a stone-quarrying business with his brother James and an uncle. Harry and James invited Walter to join them at the Malone Stone Company. Walter accepted their offer and, upon his arrival, applied his considerable accounting skills to the business. The company thrived under his financial oversight, and he was eventually appointed treasurer of the family business.

The Malone brothers' hard work and good fortune were reflected in their opulent lifestyle. They wintered in Florida, joined exclusive yachting clubs, hobnobbed with the nation's wealthiest families, including the Vanderbilts, and built fabulous mansions in Cleveland's finest neighborhoods, including along Euclid Avenue, known as "Millionaires' Row." Except for Walter. Walter's life choices were a little different from those of his wealthy kin. He was more interested in "soul winning," so he followed another life path.

After moving to Cleveland, Walter settled in with brother James and sister-in-law Caroline in their elegant home. He soon was attending Euclid Avenue Congregational Church on Sundays. Mother Mary Ann encouraged Walter to join the tiny Friends meeting house on Cedar Avenue. Instead, he involved himself in activities at the Congregational church. He conducted a boys' Sunday School class and assisted with the youth

group. Walter later referred to these experiences as his "first work" in Christian ministry.

When James and his family moved to a spacious mansion in 1881, Walter joined them and took residence in a separate wing of the grand house. Since Walter's new residence was within walking distance of the Quaker meeting house, he decided to attend a worship meeting there as his mother had long wished. That propitious decision changed the course of his life.

During his initial visit to Cleveland First Friends Church, Walter was approached in quick succession by three elderly members of the meeting, each with the same message: God was calling Walter to "take charge of the Mission Sunday School." Walter complied, believing he was Spirit-led to do so. He later remembered, "I was into the work almost before I knew it."

A year later, the little Quaker church hosted a series of revival meetings that resulted in the conversion of over one hundred souls. The revival also set the stage for the founding of Malone University. Emma Isabel Brown, along with her mother and one of her cousins, stepped foot into the church for the first time to attend the evening meetings. And they stayed. All three eventually became active members of First Friends Church. With this decision, Emma's lifelong partnership with Walter Malone was about to begin.

Born in Pickering, Ontario, in 1859 to Charles and Margaret Haight Brown, Emma moved with her family to Cleveland in 1866 and graduated as class valedictorian from the city's West Side High School. Like Walter, Emma was raised by Quaker parents, although her father, a grocery store owner, identified with a more theologically liberal branch of Friends. Margaret Brown, who had a greater spiritual influence on her daughter than Charles did, associated with the evangelical wing of Quakers.

Most of Emma's childhood was spent in a busy, multiethnic, industrial city, which was starkly different from the pastoral surroundings of Walter's youth. Her spiritual yearnings, however, were not unlike those of her future husband. In 1879, Emma attended a revival led by Dwight L. Moody, underwent a transformative conversion experience, and began to identify with evangelical Christians. Once at Cleveland First Friends Church, she joined Walter's Young People's Meeting on Sunday afternoons. Walter was much impressed with her gentle nature and spiritual insights, so he asked her to join him as co-teacher.

Emma and Walter soon discovered they were kindred spirits, so much so that they wed on January 19, 1886, in the manner of Friends, at the Cleveland meeting house. Children soon arrived. Carroll was born ten months later, followed by Walter Jr. in 1888, Esther in 1890, and Ruth in 1891. Emma gave birth to two more children after their training institute was founded: Margaret in 1894 and Franklin in 1900.

Walter and Emma's growing family and the expanding Malone Stone Company were enough to keep the couple busy, but they continued to teach and serve in a wide variety of capacities at Cleveland First Friends Church. Walter was recorded as a "Minister of the Gospel" in 1887, served as presiding clerk at the church's business meetings, was appointed to the Board of Trustees of the church, and traveled as an evangelist across the United States to other Quaker meetings. In 1889, representatives of Ohio Yearly Meeting (now Evangelical Friends Church: Eastern Region)

appointed Walter Malone as its first superintendent. Similarly, Emma was actively engaged in the life of the church and the denomination, serving as co-clerk of Ohio Yearly Meeting, a trustee of Cleveland Friends Church, and a traveling evangelist. In 1892, she too was recorded as a Friends minister.

The Malones' ministry among young adults, however, was central to their pastoral calling. Their

Young People's Meeting drew hundreds of youth from across the city and surrounding area. By the time Emma and Walter wed in 1886, over five hundred were attending their Sunday gatherings. At one point, First Friends Church contained not one classroom that could hold all of the attendees, so they met in the church sanctuary. When the church underwent a face-lift, the class was temporarily held in a nearby roller skating rink. When the remodeling project was completed and the class moved into the newly expanded sanctuary, the venue was as crowded as it had been before the renovation.

By 1891, Emma and Walter's Sunday School students were leading prayer meetings, Bible studies, and young people's classes. As the Malones watched their students mature spiritually and begin to minister to residents in Cleveland neighborhoods on their own, Walter and Emma felt themselves strongly led by the Holy Spirit to open a training school in which students could be immersed in a one-year course of study in the Bible and hands-on training "to do practical Christian work such as visiting the sick, calling in homes, and personal evangelism." Several of the young people who attended the Malones' weekly meetings were already agitating for some type of ministerial preparation, especially those who did not wish or could not afford to attend a four-year liberal arts college or seminary.

Walter and Emma were also concerned about new pedagogical approaches to Biblical studies, such as criticism of the Bible as a historical text, which were emerging at a number of Quaker

J. Walter and Emma B. Malone:
Soul Winners

The Cleveland Bible Institute, born in the heart of God, was brought to fruition through the lives of J. Walter and Emma B. Malone. It was their child; they, its parents. It was next to their hearts and dear to them as their own flesh and blood.

Rev. J. Walter Malone, blessed of the Lord, chosen of God to preach the Gospel of peace and to teach the unsearchable riches of Christ, the beloved founder of our school, has left deep on our hearts the impress of his life.

Association with Mr. Malone has been one of the precious privileges of our student days. How often the day's cares have been lifted a bit and the heart lightened by a word of encouragement or good cheer as we have passed Mr. Malone in the halls or on the grounds. Which of us has not squared his shoulders a trifle and straightened the gait a bit when we have caught the kindly twinkle of his aye as he said, "Remember the Lord and I are counting on thee." His entrance into the class room always brings a response, sometimes a hush of reverence, again a burst of song, and as one student said of him, "If the life of Christ within makes one like that, what will it be to see Jesus?"

Mrs. Malone shared fully the toil and responsibility which has made the school a success throughout its history. She gave her life's blood, her thought, her energy and her prayers for the School. She burned herself out on the altar of sacrifice which was to her a joy and delight. It was hers to pray through difficulties and hard times and get the mind of the Lord for the School. She knew how to do this, and then, too, she knew how to wait God's time for important changes.

And oh, let us never forget Mrs. Malone's loyalty to God's Word. How she loved it, how she lived by it and depended upon it and on Christ, the incarnate Word. She saw truths of the Word as matchless and sublime, truths that would stand like a rock undaunted, minding not the storms of time. Real to her were His purposes, His promises of faithfulness, of love, of grace given from above, of peace passing understanding, of mercy and of love.

~ Excerpts from the 1925 Cleveland Bible Institute catalog and the 1926 yearbook, *The Gleaner.*

colleges and post-secondary schools. The Malones believed that such teaching practices diminished the authority of Scripture and undermined an orthodox understanding of Christianity. They wanted to open an institute that was grounded in a more theologically conservative interpretation of Scripture and complemented an evangelical approach to training for domestic and foreign mission service.

Bible institutes were a fairly new phenomenon at the time. The Christian and Missionary Alliance's Missionary Training Institute, founded by A. B. Simpson and now known as Nyack College, is generally acknowledged as the first. Established in New York City in 1882, the school was the first of its kind to offer an abbreviated study of the Bible and specialized training for mission work. In 1886, Moody Bible Institute, which still prepares students for Christian service in Chicago, opened its doors to become the second urban Bible institute in the nation.

Of course, neither Walter or Emma had any experience in higher education—Bible institute or college. They were high school graduates who had never attended college or even visited a Bible institute. But they felt divinely led to pursue this calling. Given their educational background and daily responsibilities, they did not envision

themselves as instructors at their proposed school. Rather they planned to establish the school, serve as administrators, teach a course on occasion, and secure the full-time teaching services of a graduate from a trusted Quaker college.

In the meantime, Walter was asked by several Friends in 1891 to serve as president of a proposed Friends theological seminary to be located in Chicago. The seminary would be a first for Friends. Although Quakers "recorded" ministers, they never hired pastors and their meetings for worship were held in silent prayer and meditation, unless the Spirit prompted someone, whether a recorded minister or not, to speak. However, in the late 1800s, many Friends meetings were undergoing a transition from unprogrammed worship meetings to programmed worship services. Some, especially Friends situated west of the Appalachian Mountains, began to call their meeting houses "churches" and hired pastors who offered weekly sermons. Until this time, there had been no need for Friends seminaries or any type of professional training for pastors. The proposed formation of a Quaker seminary signaled a significant departure from the traditional practices of Friends.

Walter's talents as a Bible teacher and traveling evangelist were well known among Quakers throughout the United States, and he seemed to be the perfect candidate to head up a Friends seminary. However, Walter and Emma were less sure. And so, in December 1891, they retreated to their prayer closets and came away with a shared sense that the way was not open for them to move to Chicago. Yet the experience reinforced the Malones' conviction that God *was* beckoning them to found a small school for Christian workers. Three months later, they did.

The Chicago seminary never opened.

Most of the Bible institutes founded in the late nineteenth and early twentieth centuries were founded in cities, as was the Malones' school. Unbridled industrialization, urbanization, immigration, and demographic growth created a host of social and economic problems within the nation's urban centers. Bible institutes focused on ways to both evangelize among growing numbers of people in metropolitan areas and address poverty, illness, vice, and other challenges that seemed endemic to major cities.

Cleveland, Ohio, was no different. By March of 1892, with a population closing in on 300,000, Cleveland was the tenth largest city in the nation. Founded by Connecticut Yankees in 1796, Cleveland was home to a cornucopia of ethnicities in the final decade of the nineteenth century. African-Americans, Chinese, Croatians, Germans, Hungarians, Jews, Irish, Italians, Poles, Russians, Ukrainians, and descendants of the founding Yankee families populated the city. Eastern European immigrants had arrived en masse after 1870 as Cleveland became a leading industrial center and supplier of jobs. The city grew so quickly that local developers could not keep up with the housing demand. Many immigrants and migrants crowded into tenement structures and often in lived squalid conditions. The city seemed an ideal setting for a hands-on training school.

Of course, this was going to be a Quaker school like no other. While Friends schools had traditionally emphasized "practical applications" as the Malones were doing, no other Quaker institution of higher learning had yet been founded as a Bible institute or Christian training school. Furthermore, the Malones were committed to educating women alongside men, believing that all were equally called to ministry. Even more astonishing, they planned to open their doors to persons of color, long before other Quaker colleges admitted African-American students.

Opening their Christian training school seemed to be a daunting task. Nevertheless, in the early months of 1892, the Malones rented a small house on Carnegie Avenue, which was a few blocks from Cleveland First Friends Church. Members of the Malones' Young Peoples Meeting renovated the building "from attic to cellar." With the help of their Sunday School students, the Malones were soon ready for their new venture.

The opening day for the new school, initially dubbed "Christian Workers Training School for Bible Study and Practical Methods of Work," was scheduled for March 17, 1892. The date was especially fitting given J. Walter Malone's Irish heritage. Inexperienced as school administrators and concerned about the small size of the rented home, the Malones prayed, "Oh Lord, please don't let but six come." The number of students who registered on that first day? Exactly six.

The Malones hoped that Dougan Clark, an evangelist and professor of religion at Earlham College, would take charge of the one-year course of study at their new school, but he was unavailable. Clark recommended Earlham College alumna Martilla "Tilly" Cox. However, the students were uncomfortable with Cox's pedagogical style and threatened to leave the school if the Malones did not teach themselves. Cox graciously stepped down and enrolled in the training school herself. And, so, the Malones "took up the teaching," with Emma in charge of Old Testament instruction and Walter leading New Testament classes.

In addition to running the stone business in which Walter held one-third interest and overseeing a growing household, the couple conducted the school. Neither held title as "president" of the institute, but both were lead administrators and primary instructors. For the first fifteen years of the training school's existence, the Malones did not receive any compensation for themselves, but paid from their personal funds the salaries of instructors who soon joined them.

The primary purpose of the Christian Workers Training School was "soul winning" through evangelism and practical outreach. This was reflected in the school's first motto: "Out and Out for Christ." According to the 1893–94 school catalog, qualification for admission was "a desire to enter into real soul saving work." Students spent the morning in classes and the afternoon on the streets of Cleveland.

The "practical" training was centered on the near east side of Cleveland's Public Square. A veritable den of iniquity, the neighborhood hosted dozens of saloons, liquor stores, brothels, opium dens, and gambling houses. Students ministered to those in need in nursing homes, hospitals, orphanages, homeless shelters, rescue missions, and homes for unwed mothers. During the eighty-first session of Ohio Yearly Meeting, an annual conference for Ohio and Michigan Friends, Walter reported that 10,000 free meals had been provided for the local poor during the previous year. As budding evangelists, students conducted Gospel services, prayer meetings, and Bible studies.

Early on, the Malones rented the "worst theater in the city" on the second floor of the old Cleveland Music Academy. The ground floor of the

building housed four saloons, but faculty and students held evangelistic services in the theater every Wednesday and Sunday evenings. The meetings put a damper on business at the first-floor saloons, so their proprietors demanded that the Training School evangelists be evicted from the hall. They were ousted, but the theater was destroyed by fire shortly after. Reported a local paper, the theater owner "should have known better than to have let those Quakers have it, and expect to get it back."

Members of the inaugural class entered the mission field as pastors, missionaries, Sunday School teachers, and lay leaders. Esther Baird and Delia Fistler co-founded a Friends mission, school, and orphanage in India. Willis Hotchkiss, along with younger alumni Arthur and Edna Chilson and Edgar Hole, established the Friends Africa Industrial Mission in modern-day Kenya in 1902. The highest concentration of Quakers in the world is currently centered in Kenya and adjacent nations, in large part due to the missionary endeavors of these alumni. Edgar and Minnie Ellyson and Mary and Howard Moore were Friends pastors, and Nellie Thomas, Minnie Bassett, and E. Jay Lord became traveling evangelists.

By 1896, the school had grown so rapidly that the Malones temporarily closed the institution for a year until a larger instructional building could be secured. Cleveland First Friends Church provided the solution. The church members invited the Christian Workers Training School to erect an educational wing on their property. A four-story building, adjoining First Friends Church, was subsequently constructed. It accommodated fifty students and featured classrooms, dining facilities, a laundry, and a residence hall for women on the first floor and third-floor rooms for male resident students. On June 3, 1897, the building was dedicated for service, and the school was rechristened Cleveland Bible Training School.

Cleveland Bible Training School still focused on Biblical studies and practical Christian training. However, when William P. Pinkham joined the faculty in 1898, he helped strengthen the one-year course of study. The school offered elective classes in English, Greek, Hebrew, Elocution, Physical Culture, and Vocal Music. Tuition remained low, and room rent, heat, light, and fuel were free. Dining costs were $2.50 per week, and laundry fees were 25¢ per week. Both men and women served as classroom instructors, and Walter and Emma continued to share duties as principals of the school.

FIRST FRIENDS CHURCH AND BIBLE TRAINING SCHOOL, CEDAR AVENUE, CLEVELAND, OHIO.

However, the continued growth of the student body, the heavy teaching demands, and the financial burdens of the school began to weigh heavily on the Malones by the end of the century. Heretofore, their school had been a private venture. But the Malones no longer wished to go it alone administratively or financially. They wanted to partner with others who were committed to Christian education and practical training. Not surprisingly, they turned to the body of believers that had informally partnered with the Malones from the beginning: Cleveland First Friends Church.

Chapter 2: The Bible Institute (1899–1911)

Friends Bible Institute and Training School and Cleveland Bible Institute

On August 17, 1899, Walter Malone and William Pinkham, instructor of theology, submitted a letter to the monthly business meeting of Cleveland First Friends Church. The letter recounted the ways in which the training school had grown and flourished since it reopened in 1897. During that two-year span, 136 students had attended the school. They represented seven yearly meetings of Friends and at least ten denominations of the Christian faith. Of those who had completed the program, seven were missionaries, twenty were pastors, three were evangelists, three were teaching at the college level, and at least another thirty were engaged in full-time Christian service.

However, as Malone and Pinkham wrote in their letter, "A growing work like this…is attended with a large amount of labor and we feel that the burden resting upon the Principals of the School is greater than they should be expected to bear alone." The two proposed that the institution be incorporated under the laws of the State of Ohio and that oversight of the school be transferred to Cleveland Friends Church, which would then appoint a new Board of Trustees. Members of the church agreed, the state issued a new charter, and the school was renamed "Friends Bible Institute and Training School."

William Pinkham's involvement was vital during this period of this transition. Born in Maine and raised in Ohio, Pinkham was credited with systemizing and expanding the Training School's curriculum. Sharing the Malones' evangelical theology and their concern about the encroachment of liberal theology in Christian colleges and universities, Pinkham had extensive experience in Christian education. Before coming to Cleveland, he had served as principal at two Friends preparatory academies and as interim president at Earlham College in Indiana before arriving at the Malones' school in 1898. He was later appointed as president of what is now Azusa Pacific University in southern California.

And so, under the leadership of the Malones and Pinkham, the training school became a Bible institute.

Once Ohio officials approved the charter and Cleveland Friends Church agreed to help shoulder responsibility for the institute, the administration began offering a second year of training at the newly-named Friends Bible Institute and Training School (FBI). The expanded academic program still focused on the Bible and practical work in the city, but now it also offered a broader foundation in the liberal arts and music. Required courses included the Old and New Testament, Christian Doctrine, Bible History and Geography, Church History, hermeneutics and homiletics, and applied religious work. Students also registered for requisite classes in English, philosophy, speech, music, and fitness. Elective courses included introductory Hebrew and Greek. The coursework reflected the Holiness-Wesleyan and Christocentric perspective of the institute, which student Roxie Stalker characterized in 1911 as "thoroughly scriptural, practical, helpful, common sense religion." Students who fulfilled requirements for the two-year program were awarded a certificate of completion.

Friends Bible Institute
Daily Schedule (1903)

- 5:30 am Rising Bell
- 6:00 to 7:00 Family Devotions
- 7:00 to 7:30 Breakfast
- 7:30 to 8:30 Household Duties
- 8:30 to 8:45 Putting rooms in order
- 9:35 to 12:00 Classes
- 12:30 Dinner
- 2:30 to 4:25 Study or mission calls
- 4:30 to 5:20 Recitations

The students' daily schedule was packed and rather regimented. Students arose early, tended to housekeeping, and spent time in prayerful meditation during the daily Quiet Hour. Afternoons were devoted to practical religious work on Cleveland's streets and back alleys. At different periods of time, faculty and students ministered to Chinese, Jewish, Italian, and Slavic immigrants, African-American migrants, and sailors on shore leave. Students held services at city missions, evangelized in local pubs, conducted cottage prayer meetings, and engaged in house-to-house visitations. They preached on street corners and ministered in rescue missions, the city infirmary, nursing homes, and settlement houses. When the supporting denomination, Ohio Yearly Meeting of Friends, founded the Gospel City Mission on Cleveland's Erie Street in 1902, Friends Bible Institute students were among its first volunteers, and Emma Malone served as the mission's treasurer. Obviously, FBI students were rarely troubled with bouts of boredom.

However, this is why they chose to attend the Bible institute. Its holistic approach to education and evangelism was a hallmark of the FBI experience. Years later Malone's sixth president, Byron Osborne, Class of 1916, wrote, "The students of the Friends Bible Training School also demonstrated that a Christian can be evangelical in belief and also deeply concerned with what has come to be spoken of as 'social action.'"

Friends Bible Institute and Training School was particularly ambitious during the first decade of the new century. In December 1901, the school began publishing *The Soul-Winner*, a weekly religious newsletter, and founded The Soul-Winner Press. The press not only published the newsletter but also Christian tracts, pamphlets, and books. The institute purchased property adjacent to its campus to accommodate both the printing press and additional housing for male students. The school had already outgrown the 1897 building and only female students were living in the four-story structure. Male students had been residing in rented cottages nearby.

Friends Bible Institute Rules (1908–1909):

1. No visits are to be made in students' rooms during study hours or the Quiet Hour, and there should be no conversation in the halls during these hours.

2. Students are expected to come promptly to devotions, meals, and classes when the bell is rung, unless previously excused.

3. No student is excused from family worship unless prevented from attending by sickness. No one is expected to make any engagement interfering with the Students' Prayer-Meeting on Monday.

4. Students when going out for evening service should take night keys, and, on returning, go immediately and quietly to their rooms.

5. No lady student is expected to go out in the evening without permission, nor unattended. Students should not go from the building for any length of time without leaving word where they can be found, if needed.

6. Before going to breakfast the bedding should be exposed to a current of air from open window and door.

7. Students are expected to be in their rooms at 2:30 and at 7:00 p.m. for study on school days, unless engaged in mission or dining-room work.

8. On Monday there are no recitations, but extra time is given to household duties.

9. Students are expected to keep their own rooms in order, and open for inspection from 1 to 2 p.m. daily. The floor of each room must be scrubbed on every second Monday, unless covered.

10. Students must not go to the laundry or kitchen unless by permission from the matron. Not more than fifteen pieces weekly can be laundered. Laundry must be ready by 6:15 a.m. on Monday. Further rules in regard to laundry can be found in another part of the catalogue.

11. All students are expected to take exercise in the open air every day.

12. Nails, tacks and pins must on no account be put into walls.

13. Each student must attend all classes in which enrolled, unless previously excused.

14. Students are requested to refrain from loud talking, either in the home or upon the streets, and from 'foolish talking or jesting which are not convenient.'

15. Students are requested not to invite visitors to their rooms without permission from the matron.

16. Courtesy to the institution requires that students leaving the School at any other time than the close of term, should have a proper understanding with the Principals.

17. Students boarding away from the institution are expected to conform to the above rules as far as possible.

In October 1909 the Friends Bible Institute Academy, a four-year private high school, opened as an extension program of the Malones' school. The purpose of the new academy was to offer a "decidedly Christian" education in lieu of public schooling. The academy catered specifically to secondary students preparing for college. The four-year program, administered by Principal John Jenkins, included two academic tracks: classical and scientific. The academy floundered from the beginning, however, and enrollment numbers were low. Only fourteen attended during the school's first academic year and just eleven during the second. Another fifty, mostly prospective Bible institute students without high school diplomas, also enrolled in the secondary school. The academy folded in 1911, but high school-level courses were still offered until the mid-1930s for the large number of Bible institute students who lacked preparation for post-secondary coursework.

In 1910, the Alumni Association was founded. The Alumni Association raised funds for the school and kept graduates in touch with their alma mater. That same year, another new organization, the Body Guard, was established. The purpose of the Body Guard was to build the school's endowment fund, pay down school debts, and assist students with financial need. The annual membership fee was $1.00 per year, and the initial membership goal was one thousand. Many of the donations from alumni, friends of the school, churches, and other organizations were in the form of canned goods and other food stuffs. These gifts kept tuition and boarding costs in check. Both the Alumni Association and Body Guard gathered for annual banquets during Commencement Week every May.

And then, yet another name change came in 1911. Although the legal designation of the school remained Friends Bible Institute and Training School, it was rechristened Cleveland Bible Institute (CBI). This moniker appeared on all the school's materials, including the academic catalog, until 1937. Although the record does not offer a clear reason for the name change, the Bible institute was attracting increasing numbers of local residents who did not hail from a Friends church, and Cleveland was certainly more well-known than the tiny Friends denomination.

Just as the school was closing its high school academy and changing its name, Cleveland Bible Institute officials were approached about assuming operational control of a Lorain County orphanage. In 1893, John and Katie Sprunger, an Anabaptist minister and his wife, founded a home for Chicago area waifs in their hometown, Berne,

Indiana. In 1903, the couple purchased a farm near Birmingham, Ohio, and relocated their Children's Rescue Society from Berne to the northeast Ohio property. The proposed merger of the Children's Rescue Society orphanage and the Bible institute in July 1911 was precipitated by Rev. Sprunger's failing health.

Once the Bible institute began overseeing the orphanage, it was thereafter known as Children's Country Training Home. J. Walter Malone, Jr., son of Walter and Emma, served as its superintendent, and Merrill Coffin was appointed field secretary. Located on 536 rolling acres of verdant farmland on the east bank of the Vermillion River, the Children's Country Training Home offered shelter, vocational education, and spiritual training for over sixty orphaned and homeless children, many of whom came from Cleveland. The Bible institute operated the orphanage for five years,

receiving financial support from area Friends churches and Ohio Yearly Meeting until operating expenses became too burdensome. The orphanage closed, and the farm was sold.

Walter Malone, Jr. was not the only relative to come to the aid of his parents. The Bible institute and training school had always been a family affair. Three of Walter's brothers and his only sister served as trustees of the school, and son Walter Jr. was an officer of the Body Guard. Yet assistance from family members did not bring relief to the overextended Malones.

Emma and Walter found it difficult to curb their activities. In the midst of their expanding administrative responsibilities at the school, the Malones accepted appointments as senior co-pastors of Cleveland First Friends Church in 1908, a position they held until 1917. Furthermore, they continued to travel as evangelists and denominational representatives to churches and revival meetings across the United States. In time, the burdensome duties began to take a toll on the Malones' health. Both became frail and sickly, and they often traveled to the Florida homes of Walter's brothers to rejuvenate. Still, it became apparent that they could no longer carry the heavy load.

And so, twenty-six years after they founded the school, Walter and Emma stepped down as co-principals in 1918. But they didn't retire. Walter carried on as president of the Board of Trustees, Emma remained treasurer of the board, and both continued to teach classes. They were assigned new titles: Counsellors of the Bible institute. Alumnus Edgar A. Wollam, a veteran faculty member, was named Executive Secretary of the school and Edward Mott, having first been appointed as Dean in 1916, continued in that position. Shortly thereafter, Edgar Wollam's title was changed to "President," the first chief administrator of the institute to be so designated.

Even before Wollam took the helm, the Bible institute's student population was expanding during the early years of the new century. By the fall of 1902, 150 students were enrolled at the school. A recession in 1907 led to a sixty percent drop in enrollment between 1902 and 1908, but enrollment steadily increased over the next ten years. By 1920, over two hundred students were attending CBI annually.

Although Edgar Wollam had long served as a faculty member and administrator, his tenure as president was brief, stepping down as president after only three years. Under his leadership, the focus, mission, and curriculum remained the same. President Wollam was as committed to "soul winning" as the Malones. Wollam often led evangelistic services throughout the city and was usually accompanied by a fifty-voice student choir. Students continued to minister in hospitals, prisons, and the local boys' reformatory. They served as pastors, evangelists, and Sunday School teachers while in school and upon graduating. Soloists and quartets provided special music at churches and religious meetings. Practical religious work remained central and was directed by new faculty member Byron L. Osborne, son-in-law of Walter and Emma Malone and husband to their daughter Ruth.

Perhaps the most memorable, and frightening, event during Wollam's presidency was the influenza pandemic that forced the closure of all Cleveland-area schools, churches, and businesses in October 1918. Before he resigned in 1921 to pastor a Friends Church in Kansas, President Wollam implemented two notable changes. Cleveland Bible Institute moved from a three-term to a two-semester academic year and, even more significantly, began to offer a three-year course of study.

When Wollam resigned, the Malones were at a loss over how they might identify a suitable successor. The post-World War I recession had contributed to a fifty percent decline in student enrollment and a deepening financial crisis. These challenges created a dire need for a capable and

astute administrator. But, where to find one? Fortunately, the Malones were well-connected to a larger evangelical network. In fact, CBI regularly invited a dozen or more special speakers, Quaker and non-Quaker, to campus annually. One of the more dynamic visitors was evangelist and Methodist pastor, Rev. Charles W. Butler, D. D., from Detroit, Michigan. Walter and Emma traveled to Butler's hometown and invited him to assume leadership of the school with the title of Dean. Dr. Butler's willingness to serve as both administrator and faculty member came as a great relief to the Malones. After what was most likely a trial period, Butler was eventually appointed President of the Bible institute in 1923.

Butler's fifteen-year tenure was not an easy one. The lingering postwar economic slump and the Great Depression a decade later were formidable problems. In time, Dr. Butler's steady hand helped stabilize enrollment and within the first few years of his presidency, the school raised forty thousand dollars to pay off the institute's debt and invest in needed improvements. Yet the financial health of the school remained precarious with the onset of the Great Depression, and this situation was compounded by the changing economic landscape of the Cedar Avenue neighborhood. When the school first moved to Cedar Avenue, the area was primarily residential. By the mid-1930s, locals referred to the district

as "the roaring third precinct" because it was increasingly plagued by crime and vice. Coupled with the economic downturn and Cleveland First Friends Church congregation's decision to move to East Cleveland in 1932, the future outlook for Cleveland Bible Institute appeared to be dim.

In 1930 Vice President Byron Osborne organized a "Fellowship of Intercession" to begin the process of finding a new location for CBI, but no property was either available or suitable. The Board of Trustees considered closing the school at one point, but, happily, enough trustees wavered, and CBI remained open. As Osborne noted at the time, "The work of Cleveland Bible Institute MUST go forward. It cannot be that the Lord no longer has a place for this School." Significant donations and the willingness of some of the teachers and administrators to forego their salaries temporarily kept CBI afloat. Enrollment remained fairly constant, if never robust, throughout the 1930s.

The small size of the institute meant that faculty members, including the president, wore a number of hats. Marian Pratt was a case in point. A public school teacher before graduating from CBI in 1919, Pratt was appointed at various times as registrar, preceptress (overseer of moral conduct), secretary of the Board of Trustees, member of the Board's executive, finance, and housekeeping committees, chair of the Education Department, and instructor of church history, the Bible, homiletics,

psychology, logic, and pedagogy between 1919 and her departure in 1936. In 1925 and 1926, she even served as president of the Alumni Association. While Pratt may have fulfilled more roles than any other faculty member or administrator in the history of Malone University and its antecedents, she was not alone in serving in a wide range of capacities. Such were the challenges of the tiny Bible institute.

Like Pinkham before him, Butler was intent on expanding and invigorating the curriculum. During the Butler years, the institute offered five courses of study: the basic three-year theological course; a four-year theological course, which included one year of preparatory work for those who had not finished high school; Christian Workers' Bible Course, an abbreviated program for non-traditional students; the two-year Gospel Singers Course for those with callings in music ministry; and the short-lived post-graduate course of study, which was offered on demand. Coursework alone did not set the Bible institute apart. Conduct mattered too.

As was the case at most Bible institutes, colleges, and universities at the time, CBI applied *in loco parentis* (Latin for "in place of a parent") to its relationship with its students, whether of legal age or not. Deportment at Cleveland Bible Institute was "measured by Scriptural stands, the ideal being the love that doth not behave unseemly," as noted in the school's annual catalogs. A student's conduct was deemed important enough to be appraised by faculty when determining candidacy for graduation.

CBI students were required to attend church services on Sunday mornings and afternoons, daily chapel, and Monday night prayer services. In addition, students were expected to meditate and pray during the daily Quiet Hour. They were also required to abide by strict rules of conduct when courting. Young men were granted permission to escort women to their homes if their female companions lived off-campus. Courting couples enjoyed social privileges in the school's parlor on either Saturday or Sunday from 2:00 to 5:00 p.m., although couples engaged to be married were not permitted to wed during the school year. Students who failed to comply with CBI regulations appeared before the faculty and were then directed to apologize to the entire student body. Those who committed the most egregious infractions were expelled. However, given that these behavioral parameters were common at most institutions of higher learning, CBI students expected no less.

Although packed with classes and field work, life at CBI was not without its amusements and opportunities for spiritual growth. A number of clubs and organizations kept students busy. Early on, students at the institute joined the larger Student Volunteer Movement, a national organization that supported foreign mission work and prepared students for service abroad. After World War I, the Student Volunteer club at CBI was replaced by the Missionary Band. Missionary Band members raised money for a mission in China, volunteered to teach English to Chinese immigrants at the Old Stone Church in downtown Cleveland, and invited missionaries to speak on campus. The Gleaners Association, founded in 1923, focused on domestic evangelism. Student groups canvassed the surrounding neighborhoods, conducted Bible schools and Sunday School class, and published a newsletter, *The Student Messenger*, chronicling their evangelistic efforts. Since music instruction was required, men and women participated in the school choir, orchestra, and a variety of instrumental and vocal groups. Other organizations included a literary club and two groups, the Odd Jobs Club and the Service Club, assisted male and female students,

respectively, in securing employment. Off-campus employment helped them finance their schooling and living expenses.

Students enjoyed lighter moments as well. The school catalog boasted of its location in one of the leading cities in the United States. Cleveland was home to the third largest public library in the nation, the world-renowned Cleveland Orchestra, and one of the finest art museums in the country. The lakeside metropolis, nicknamed the "Forest City" as early as 1834, also had an extensive park system. Wade Park, which eventually became home to Cleveland's cultural center, drew nearby CBI students on Saturday and Sunday afternoons.

Of course, given that a disproportionate number of CBI students hailed from isolated rural locations, the urban locale also offered students an "opportunity to escape from that provincialism which too often limits the influence of the Christian worker," explained CBI's promotional materials. Cleveland's ethnic diversity, cultural amenities, and variety of social and service opportunities not only prepared students for Christian ministry at home and abroad, but also enhanced their own cultural experiences while at CBI.

Cleveland Bible Institute students certainly took advantage of the city's offerings. Ruth Lawton Thurston of Rhode Island wrote about life at Cleveland Bible Institute in 1926. After a weekend lunch during the winter months, she remembered, "a crowd goes off joyously, wearing sweaters and caps, with their skates slung over their shoulders. Another group similarly attired goes off for a hike in the glorious winter air, and still another goes downtown for their weekly shopping." The frivolity continued on campus after dinner, when students gathered in the parlor for games and sweet treats prepared by the students in the school's kitchen. Thurston even recounted nighttime rituals with fondness: "Ten o'clock comes all too soon, and it is with reluctance that the retiring bell is obeyed. The lights are out, and the CBI dormitories have settled down to the quiet of another night. The student turned comfortably in bed, and the last waking thought was, 'What a good place CBI is to be in, and how glad I am that I am here!'" Freshmen and senior receptions, holiday celebrations, and school picnics rounded out the festivities.

Of course, for all the chaste entertainment offered by the school, Cleveland Bible Institute officials were primarily concerned with preparing men and women for effective Christian service. Indeed, during the Butler era, the school was fast gaining a national reputation as a theologically trustworthy Christian training school. Long before *U.S. News & World Report* began to publish its annual college rankings, the editorial staff at *The Sunday School Times* printed its own list of the nation's most reputable Bible institutes in 1924. Under the heading "Biblical Institutes That Are Sound," *The Sunday School Times* implored parents and prospective students to attend one of forty-two recommended schools, including Cleveland Bible Institute, to safeguard their "spiritual health." In

1930 *The Christian Fundamentalist* published an up-dated roster of stalwart Bible institutes. Cleveland Bible Institute was among the twenty-eight schools included on both lists. Although tiny in size, by the end of President Butler's tenure in 1936, CBI was firmly established as a leading Bible institute in the nation.

As early as 1928, President Butler began to relinquish some of his CBI duties when he was elected president of the National Association for the Promotion of Holiness (NAPH). With the permission of the Board of Trustees, Butler delegated many of his responsibilities to Vice President Osborne. In addition to traveling on behalf of the NAPH, Butler took up the pulpit at his church in Detroit, traveling home every weekend. Although he returned half of his salary back to the institute, Butler's personal schedule was grueling, and the school's finances were again in disarray due to the Great Depression and outdated methods of accounting. As already recounted, the school remained open during the leanest years, but Dr. Butler eventually made the decision to resign and assume the presidency of John Fletcher College, another holiness Bible institute, in Iowa. Years later Osborne characterized the departing president: "Dr. Butler was rarely gifted to teaching doctrine and, with his strong and winning personality, left a deep impression on the minds of his students."

Charles W. Butler's move to Iowa in 1936 marked the end of an era in more ways than one. Both Emma and Walter Malone passed away during Butler's presidency. Walter and Emma had always been frail physically, but the competing demands of the school, their family, Cleveland First Friends Church, and the stone business, which eventually folded, took a toll. Shortly after what they had hoped would be a restorative trip to the Florida homes of Walter's brothers, Emma Malone succumbed to illness on May 9, 1924. After his wife's death, Walter lived with daughter Ruth Malone Osborne and her family in their East Cleveland home. Walter, who was dubbed "The Saint" by his students in 1926, stepped down as a faculty member and president of the Board of Trustees in 1929. He was honored with the titles "Teacher Emeritus" and "President Emeritus" by the board. Crippled with disease, Walter died on December 30, 1935. His final blessing, recorded by family members, was in part, "May the Lord's special blessing be upon you all, and may you one and all earnestly seek the Lord while He may be found, and without fail call upon him while He is near."

For the first time in the school's history, neither Walter or Emma Malone were involved in the life of the institution they had established over forty years before. Under their watch, the program of study at their diminutive school had evolved from a one-year course to a three-year program, the student population had grown twenty-five-fold, and administrative leadership had changed two times. Their legacy would bolster and preserve the school in the years to come.

As the Bible institute era was drawing to a close, a new president was about to be inaugurated, and the Board of Trustees would soon consider yet another revision of the school's curriculum. Students rarely arrived anymore without the requisite high school diploma, and only a handful still needed the one-year preparatory course before commencing the three-year course of study. Thus, it was time to phase out the preparatory year and add a fourth year of coursework.

The Bible college era was about to begin.

Chapter 3: The Bible College (1937–1956)

Cleveland Bible College

In the summer of 1948, Lois Seward of Burbank, Ohio, wrote a cheery note to an incoming freshman, Dolores Stratton of Salem, Ohio. Seward, who would soon be serving as sophomore class secretary, was a participant in the popular "Big Sister-Little Sister" program at Cleveland Bible College, and she had been matched with Stratton as her "little sister" for the upcoming academic year. "Welcome to our C.B.C. family," Seward wrote, "I can truly say that last year was one of the happiest, most thrilling years of my life preparing to do the work of the Lord. Each day brings loads of blessings."

The Cleveland Bible College years, which lasted for nearly two decades, continued to fulfill the Malones' desire to prepare men and women "to do the work of the Lord." The CBC era can also be seen as a bridge between the relatively narrow academic scope of the Bible institute and the broader curriculum of the liberal arts college that followed. Cleveland Bible College was not alone in this transformative process. A number of Bible institutes across the nation were reconstituted as Bible colleges around the same time, and some, including CBC, began offering a wide menu of liberal arts courses.

The Bible college era was one of significant change. Three presidents served the institution during this period, a junior college curriculum was added, and, after fourteen years of searching for a suitable property, the school finally moved from its Cedar Avenue home. Regardless of the shift in leadership or campus location, Cleveland Bible College remained an exemplar of its type: theologically conservative, pietistic, and focused on the global mission of the church.

∾ ∾

With the departure of Charles W. Butler as president of Cleveland Bible Institute in 1936, the Board of Trustees was tasked with identifying a new chief administrator. As was the case with President Edgar Wollam, the trustees found their new president close to home. Like Wollam, Worthy A. Spring was an alumnus of the school. A 1926 graduate of Cleveland Bible Institute and a member of its Board of Trustees, President Spring had been serving as pastor at United Brethren churches in eastern Ohio before his appointment. His familiarity with the school, his commitment to its mission, and his experience as a church administrator made for a good fit.

Once Rev. Spring was appointed to the post, the structure of the Board of Trustees was slightly modified. Heretofore, the lead administrator or president of the institution typically served as president of the Board of Trustees as well. That practice ended with the Spring presidency. Charles E. Haworth, board member from 1919 to 1932, was

reappointed in 1936 and served as president of the Board of Trustees from 1937 until 1959, one of the board's longest serving presidents in the school's history. Members of the Board of Trustees were no longer exclusively drawn from Cleveland First Friends Church as had been the case in 1899, but they were predominantly Friends. Of the eighteen trustees, twelve were appointed by Ohio Yearly Meeting and six hailed from other evangelical denominations. One of the six was nominated by the Alumni Association.

More changes were on the horizon. In March 1937, less than a year after Spring came on board and after "years of praying and planning," the Board of Trustees authorized the "raising of the academic standards to college rank" and rechristened the school yet again, this time as Cleveland Bible College. CBC officials deemed the move a logical step and likened the transition to a number of

preparatory academies that had become liberal arts colleges in the nineteenth century. More importantly, a baccalaureate degree enabled prospective pastors and other Christian workers,

especially those who were unable or did not wish to enroll in seminary after graduation, to secure pastoral positions that required advanced training.

The curriculum was thoroughly revamped. A four-year Bible course leading to a Bachelor of Theology degree replaced the two existing Bible and theology tracks. The new program not only required a fourth year of study, but Th.B. students were also expected to write and defend a two- to four-thousand-word thesis. The three-year Gospel Singers and Christian Workers courses of study initially remained intact. No thesis was required for these two majors, although students enrolled in diploma programs were required to prepare and deliver an oration.

College administrators assured their various constituencies that the institution was holding firm to its "original calling to train and equip Christian workers for service." Noted the 1937–38 college catalog, "Cleveland Bible College is dedicated to the sacred task of sending forth laborers into the harvest. This being the case, only those students are admitted who have experienced the saving grace of Christ and who desire better to fit themselves to serve Him." As noted in the previous chapter, since increasing numbers of applicants had already earned their high school diploma when matriculating at the school, the institution phased out the preparatory year for those who had not. Thereafter, a high school diploma, or at least fifteen high school credits, became a prerequisite for admission.

Ten years later, the curriculum underwent another significant revision. In 1947, the Board of Trustees approved a two-year "Junior College" for students who did not aspire to full-time Christian service but still desired to attend a Christian institution of higher learning. The Junior College offered liberal arts courses as well as Bible classes. Students could then transfer their general education credits after two years at CBC or upon completion of the Th.B. to a four-year liberal arts college. Trustees dropped both the Gospel Singers and Christian Workers certificate programs at that time and added a Bachelor of Sacred Music degree.

As a newly-minted Bible college in 1937, CBC focused more intentionally on expanding its library holdings. From five hundred volumes in the early 1930s to 3,500 volumes in 1940, the library housed over seven thousand by 1950. A year later, the library director adopted the Dewey Decimal System for cataloging the library's resources, a system that remained in place throughout the institution's history.

Although the college was accredited by the Department of Education of the State of Ohio, Cleveland Bible College was not recognized by any independent accreditation agency. This was in part because an accrediting organization specific to Bible colleges did not exist until the Accrediting Association of Bible Institutes and Bible Colleges was formed in 1947. As one of its first members, Cleveland Bible College applied for provisional acceptance into membership on the collegiate level. The school was fully accredited within two years. In 1953 the Accrediting Association of Bible Institutes and Bible Colleges recommended that the Th.B. degree be expanded to a five-year program, and CBC officials complied. Students who enrolled in the four-year program earned a Bachelor of Religious Education degree instead of the Th.B.

Throughout the CBC era, guest lecturers and special speakers continued to supplement the college's offerings. During the 1938–39 academic year alone, sixty-three lecturers, missionaries, evangelists, and musicians spoke or performed on campus. The curriculum changes and external speakers all primed the school for its transition to a liberal arts college in the years to come.

With the shift from an institute to a college, enrollment figures began to tick upward, especially as the Great Depression came to an end. The number of students attending the school increased by thirty-one percent during Cleveland Bible College's first year, from 107 to 155 students. Enrollment figures remained fairly steady through the war years with enrollment at 192 by 1945. The student body jumped forty-one percent the following year when CBC reintroduced a long defunct night school. Almost all the students attending classes in the evening were from Cleveland, which is not surprising given the college's location

and the city's growing population. Regardless, even without night and part-time students included in the mix, the number of traditional students attending CBC continued to grow. By the time Cleveland Bible College held its final commencement in 1956, over three hundred students were enrolling annually.

Like most Bible colleges, CBC was decidedly evangelical in its theology and required its students to reflect a similar religious outlook. Students were expected to adopt the central tenets of the school: the centrality of an "experiential knowledge of pardon and regeneration," baptism by the Holy Spirit, a continual and deepening prayer life, and personal dedication to a life of Christian service. Behavioral expectations on and off campus remained fairly constrained compared to current conventions, although CBC's prescribed standards of decorum were common at most private and public colleges during that time period.

Women were especially subject to particular guidelines regarding proper attire. Perhaps because fashion for women had radically changed after World War I, in 1938, for the first time, college officials deemed it necessary to publish a "Standard of Dress for Bible College Women" in its annual catalog. No equivalent standard of dress was articulated for male students, but that was also fairly typical at the midpoint of the last century.

In some ways, Cleveland Bible College was an incubator, a protected environment that attended to the spiritual training and care of its students. And that was the point. Students intentionally chose to enroll at CBC to prepare for "Gospel service," and they clearly flourished. Michigan native Howard W. Moore, a member of the Class of 1946, affirmed the words of CBC officials when characterizing his own years as a student. The value of his Cleveland Bible College education, Dr. Moore noted, was the "study of the Bible, rather than merely learning facts about the Bible. It is to search

Standard of Dress for Bible College Women (1938)

- Cleveland Bible College is a Christian school, and as such seeks to maintain the highest standards of simplicity, modesty, and refinement with regard to the dress of its young women.
- Therefore, we require that young women avoid extremely sheer dress materials, and that all sleeves shall come at least to the elbow, preferably below.
- Skirts shall be well below the knees. We desire to conform to Bible teaching, the standard being "that women adorn themselves in modest apparel, with shamefacedness and sobriety" (I Timothy 2:9, 10).
- "Clothing is beautiful only as it is expressive of noble character."

out, using sound principles of hermeneutics, to discover what God intended the first hearers of His message to receive, and then apply the Truth personally."

Edward L. Mitchell, M.D., Class of 1951, echoed Moore's sentiments. "The Cleveland Bible College experience for me was life changing," remembered the Virginia native. "There, I expanded my understanding and love for the Word of God. There, I found fellowship with other students who knew how to pray and to share Christ. There, God gave me my life verse, Matthew 6:33. There,

I won the heart of Ruth Alma [Mosher], my wonderful wife. There, I also heard God calling me to become a physician and to preach my way through pre-med, medical school, and surgical training. I say, 'Praise the Lord for Cleveland Bible College!'" Mitchell's life verse, which reads: "But seek first his kingdom and his righteousness, and all these things will be given to you as well," was later etched on the cornerstone of the eponymous Mitchell Hall, which was constructed on the Canton campus in 1999.

Clubs and activities reflected the missional outlook of CBC students. The Missionary League, the Gleaners, and the Soul-Winners Club were among the largest student organizations during the Bible college era. The Missionary League hosted an annual Missionary Conference, organized a missionary prayer band, and eventually supported three alumni on the mission field. When Professor John Grafton, Class of 1930, was appointed a faculty member in 1937, he took charge of the Practical Work Department, later known as the Christian Service Department. Under his oversight, members of the Soul-Winners Club took to the streets of Cleveland, preaching and ministering to local residents, as Emma and Walter Malone's pupils had done before them. CBC students could be found in churches, rescue hospitals, missions, or "any place where people are hungry for the gospel."

Music was a central feature in each of the baccalaureate programs, as well as the college's overall evangelistic efforts. All students were

required to enroll in music classes and participate in the college chorus. Sacred Music majors were also required to take chalk art classes as another means by which to evangelize. The school had long fielded an orchestra, and a select choir was added in 1945. A variety of smaller groups performed at conferences, churches, religious camps, and revival services, and on campus. Some of the names of the musical groups seem quaint in retrospect, including the Royal Sons, the Royal Daughters, Quakerettes, Gospelaires, Soldiers of the Cross, King's Four, Holy Crusaders Chorus, and Trumpeteers. Yet their evangelistic reach extended well beyond Cedar Avenue.

In fact, it was not uncommon for Bible college students to participate in more than one traveling ensemble. Virginia native Clifton Robinson, President of the Class of 1941, was a member of the Royal Sons Quartet from 1938 to 1940. Later, Robinson formed a musical duet, the Robinson-Osborne Evangelistic Party, with his future brother-in-law, trombonist B. Lindley Osborne, for two years. Howard Moore and Curtis Chambers, President of the Class of 1946, were part of a male quartet. They also traveled as a ministry team for four years. After graduating from CBC, Moore and Chambers kept their ministry team intact while attending seminary in Kentucky. For seven years, the two collaborated as music and preaching evangelists.

Another avenue of evangelism was a Sunday morning radio program. First broadcast over WDOK, a Cleveland radio station, in 1952, the "Word of the King" hour featured music by Cleveland Bible College students and a Sunday school lesson hosted by Byron Osborne. By the end of the Bible college era, the "Word of the King" was being broadcast via eight radio stations in Indiana, Michigan, Ohio, and Virginia.

The school still made the most of its urban setting, which opened a vast array of educational, recreational, and evangelistic doors for Cleveland Bible College students. "The College has a distinctive purpose in her location," wrote President Spring in 1937. "She is in the midst of a very needy field, in which she expects to do a great work of evangelism among children and adults. The large city provides scores of opportunities for those in training to put into practice their methods and their consecration. Furthermore, being centrally located, her students find easy accessibility to their places of employment, for a number of them work to defray expenses."

While tuition and living expenses were quite low compared to fees in the coming century, college costs could be daunting for CBC students. During the 1940–1941 academic year, tuition for commuting students was $35 per semester and $25 per semester for residential students. Residents paid $80 for table board and $38 for room rent every semester, or $286 in total for the year. By the time Cleveland Bible College moved to a quarter system in 1948, overall costs reflected

post-war inflationary pressures. Students were charged $37.50 per quarter for tuition, although students who opted out of "Domestic Duty" paid $64.00 per quarter. Residents paid $100 for table board and between $27.50 and $37.50 for room rent, depending on single or double occupancy. Yearly tuition, room, and board costs ranged from $495 to $604.50, not including matriculation, music, laundry, and other fees. As would continue to be the case into the next century, students at the Malones' school typically worked on or off campus to cover educational costs.

Once the institute became a college, school officials added a number of accoutrements often associated with college life. Shortly before the transition to a Bible college, the first student newspaper, *The Voice*, was founded. A new college yearbook, the *CleBiCo*, was first published in 1937 and every year thereafter through 1956, except for the 1939 yearbook, which was entitled *The Reaper*. Beginning in 1941, the Gleaners hosted an annual youth conference at the school, which doubled both as an evangelistic opportunity and a recruiting tool. Student Council was introduced during the 1946–47 academic year, and an annual Homecoming celebration was first observed in October 1951. As had been done for several years, *The Messenger* published college updates for alumni and friends of the school.

There were a variety of social clubs in which students participated. Most had a decidedly Bible college twist. The Dormitory Prayer Band for male and female residents and the Day Girls'

Prayer Band for commuting women brought students together for collective prayer, meditation, and worship. The Southerner's Club was comprised of students from Virginia and North Carolina, where a number of Friends Churches were located. North Carolina native Byron Osborne served as club advisor. One of the quirkier organizations was the Bachelor Men's Club for unmarried and unattached men. Although intercollegiate athletics were not introduced until the school moved to Canton, intramural sports became a recreational staple at Cleveland Bible College. Athletic offerings were initially limited to men's basketball and co-ed volleyball, but baseball, football, and horseshoes were soon added. The annual horseshoe competition was a favorite event, and the champion was honored with a school trophy. Each of these clubs and activities enriched and enhanced college life, and graduating students carried away with them lifelong memories.

Perhaps the most momentous change in the nineteen-year history of Cleveland Bible College was the move to a new location in 1945. From the time of his appointment as chair of the Fellowship of Intercession by the Board of Trustees in 1930, Professor Osborne had been praying with three hundred other members of the Fellowship for a new campus home. Attempts to purchase property in Cleveland or Cleveland Heights fell through due to a shortage of funds or zoning restrictions. Tentative offers of major gifts to finance a relocation were never realized. Disappointed, some members of the Fellowship of Intercession quietly withdrew. Although the school had purchased the old First Friends Church building four years after the congregation moved to its East Cleveland location in 1932, the Cedar Road facilities were no longer adequate. Finally, fourteen years after the Fellowship was formed, a potential site three blocks away became available.

In the fall of 1944, a three-acre property at 3201 Euclid Avenue was put up for sale at a list price of $125,000. The lot included a majestic mansion, built during the heyday when Euclid Avenue was known as "Millionaires' Row," a three-story classroom structure that had originally lodged servicemen during World War II, and a utility building. During the waning years of the war, a business school began leasing the property, but its administrators decided to vacate the site shortly thereafter. With $30,000 in its relocation fund, CBC bid $100,000 for the property. The Warren Cornell family, which owned the site, agreed to the price, and school officials immediately drafted plans for removal to the new location.

On May 31, 1945, Cleveland Bible College's new campus was dedicated. A year later, the college purchased the Chisholm mansion, which was situated at 2827 Euclid Avenue, a few blocks west

of the main campus. It was repurposed as the women's residence hall and named in honor of alumna Esther Baird, member of the first graduating class and a missionary to India. Additional apartment buildings were acquired or retained from the old campus to accommodate male and married students. Thus began the school's twelve-year stint on Euclid Avenue.

After a dozen years at the helm, President Spring's tenure came to an end in 1948 when he was appointed president of Kletzing College in University Park, Iowa. His replacement was George Hodgin, a Friends minister and recently retired professor at Asbury College. Hodgin was the first Quaker appointed to the post in twenty-seven years. A former missionary with his wife Jennie and chair of the board of directors of the World Gospel Mission, his stint as president was brief. Hodgin resigned in 1951. When searching for a new president, the Board of Trustees turned to another alumnus, a Quaker minister, and the most senior member of the Cleveland Bible College staff at the time: Byron L. Osborne.

President Osborne, Class of 1916, was first appointed as an instructor at Cleveland Bible Institute in 1920. Shortly after graduating from CBI, he had married Emma and Walter's second eldest daughter, Ruth, in 1917, and the couple moved to Virginia where they pastored a Friends church before returning to Cleveland. They raised their family in East Cleveland, and all four of their children, Ruth "Betty" Elizabeth, Emma "Gerrie" Geraldine, Byron Lindley, and Hendricks Malone, attended Cleveland Bible College. Betty's husband, Clifton Robinson, served briefly as the school's Director of Promotions. Gerrie's husband, John Williams, taught for several years at the school

and directed the technology courses and radio program. Except for Walter and Emma Malone and Jack Hazen, few labored faithfully for as many years at the Malones' school as Byron Osborne. Although Dr. Osborne had been passed over for the post at least once before, to the dismay of some, he made the most of his nine years as president of the school his in-laws had founded.

Deeply respectful of the legacy of Emma and Walter Malone, Osborne hoped to keep the "spiritual note prominent" at Cleveland Bible College. He encouraged students to observe the Quiet Hour and tend to their personal devotions more faithfully. Osborne preserved the tradition of Founders Week, during which religious services were held in mid-March. He inaugurated Cleveland Bible College Homecoming Day in 1951 and later invited J. Walter Malone, Jr., President of Milliken University, to be a featured Homecoming speaker. By the time the school celebrated its sixtieth anniversary in 1952, over twelve hundred students had graduated from the college, alumni were serving in the United States and around the world, and six Bible institutes or colleges had been "mothered directly or indirectly" by Cleveland Bible College. "I do not need to remind you," Osborne told the Board of Trustees in 1952 "that our prosperity and usefulness as a Bible college is contingent upon our keeping the blessing of God upon the institution."

Although Cleveland Bible College was a fairly self-contained spiritual and educational haven, the CBC community was not immune to the impact of global political events and socio-cultural trends. The waning years of the Great Depression and World War II consumed the nation during the Bible college era. Frugality was foremost on the minds of students and faculty during the economic downturn and the Second World War. To help keep students well-nourished during this time of scarcity, Friends churches donated fruit, vegetables, and canned goods to the school throughout the Bible college era.

World War II presented its own set of moral challenges. Although the Friends denomination was historically a peace church and supported its members who registered and served as conscientious objectors, it remained steadfastly loyal to its "beloved country." Ministerial students were exempt from the draft, so the institution's male enrollment was not as affected as was often the case at liberal arts and technical colleges. After the war ended in 1945, veterans were warmly welcomed at Cleveland Bible College. The school was listed as an approved institution for which veterans who were eligible under the Serviceman's Readjustment Act of 1944 could receive educational funding. The 1950–51 annual college catalog advertised its open door in bold letters: "Approved for Veterans."

The return of veterans also signaled the start of the marriage and baby booms in the postwar period. This was no less true at Cleveland Bible College. The average age at marriage for men and women dropped significantly after World War II. By the end of the CBC era, nearly fifty percent of all brides married by the age of nineteen. Wedding fever infected the Bible college as well. Beginning with its 1945 edition, the *CleBiCo* featured wedding photographs of its undergraduates and graduating seniors. Ten wedding portraits were included in the 1947 yearbook alone. Future Malone College professor Gene Collins and wife Carolyn Adams Collins were captured in their wedding finery in the final edition of the *CleBiCo* in 1956.

The institution continued to welcome students of color, and a small but significant number of CBC scholars were African American. Although the racial composition of the student body is not clearly delineated in extant college records, the proportion of black students reached nearly ten percent on occasion. While the percentage of minority students was typically lower than that in any given year, African-American students served as class officers, participated in clubs and intramural sports, and partnered with their classroom peers as evangelists.

However, the presence of a relatively diverse student population was not without its challenges. In 1949, the secretary of the Cleveland chapter of the National Association for the Advancement of Colored People sent a letter to President Hodgin, expressing concern over reports of a possible "separation" of black and white students on campus. While it is not clear if such a plan was ever informally articulated, it was never official college policy. President Hodgin reported at the time that one black student in particular had been disrespectful to college officials, although the entire episode was evidently precipitated by a chapel speaker who used "derogatory language in reference to race."

At the dawn of the Civil Rights Movement, CBC officials sometimes found it difficult, as did their counterparts at other institutions of higher learning, to understand fully the turbulent waters that minority students navigated.

Faculty members faced their own struggles. Even with the growing number of students, faculty salaries were quite low. As a result, it was difficult to attract professors with advanced degrees, so only a handful had earned more than a baccalaureate degree. Only five of the twelve faculty members, including President Osborne, had earned graduate degrees by 1952. None had earned doctorates, although Osborne received an honorary doctoral degree from Taylor University in 1950. To complicate matters, most faculty members could not afford suitable housing. President Osborne appealed to the Board of Trustees to address the issue. "For years a crying need at the Bible College has been for adequate housing for the married men on our faculty. These men have almost been compelled to take pastorates in order to have a house in which to rent or to buy," Osborne bemoaned. Interestingly enough, President Osborne did not mention the housing plight of female faculty, but this may have been because most were single, living on campus, or married to male faculty members. In response to this crisis, the college purchased twenty acres of land in 1953 in nearby Brecksville on which to construct faculty homes. Within a year, Professor John Williams and his growing brood were living in the house that came with the Brecksville property, two more houses

were being constructed, and a community vegetable garden was in the works. In time, the school established a loan program to help faculty members purchase housing.

Although the Bible college had struggled with finances over the years, President Osborne launched a campaign in 1952 to pay off the school's $70,000 mortgage obligation by June 1, 1953. His efforts were successful and, eight years after purchasing the Euclid Avenue campus, the college community held a "mortgage burning ceremony" during Commencement week in 1953. The debt was paid. With a relatively new campus home, measures to provide housing for the faculty, and its finances on solid footing, the college's future seemed to be settled.

The reprieve did not last long.

In 1955, President Osborne received word that the State Highway Department was preparing to seize the Esther Baird Hall property for a public project. The Baird Hall parcel was needed to make way for what is now Interstate 90. Unfortunately, there was not enough space on the main campus to construct enough housing to compensate for the loss of Baird Hall. What to do?

College officials initially had no intention of leaving Cleveland and explored a number of possibilities to remain in the city. Even before the school was informed about the freeway project, officials sought to purchase another large plot of land on Euclid Avenue, which had been used for a technical school. Alas, the deal fell through in 1954. President Osborne proposed that the

school exchange its Euclid Avenue campus with the defunct U.S. Marine Hospital on Fairhill Road in Cleveland, which had recently been designated as surplus government property. To the dismay of CBC officials, the plan was rejected by the agency in charge of disposing of the hospital. Efforts to purchase the Fairhill Road property and another site on nearby Chester Avenue were still in the works when the Board of Trustees met on October 19, 1955, to consider its options. During the meeting, trustee Lambert Huffman, a member of Canton First Friends Church, suggested a move to Canton, a small city situated sixty miles south of the Bible college campus.

While a move from the Euclid Avenue campus was clearly unavoidable, board members were reluctant to leave Cuyahoga County. After all, Cleveland had been the school's home for all of its sixty-three years, and CBC had recently purchased the Brecksville land to accommodate faculty housing. Instead, the board voted to take another look at the Marine Hospital and temporarily tabled a decision to move beyond Cleveland's borders. The college did submit a bid on the Fairhill Road property, but by December 1955 it was clear that the U.S. government preferred that the facility continue to be used for medical purposes.

With all options for a quick purchase of Cuyahoga County property coming to a close and the deadline for vacating Baird Hall looming over them, the trustees were newly receptive to alternative locations. With Board approval, Osborne and Huffman met with Canton and Stark County officials to learn more about a fifty-acre parcel situated on 25th Street near the northern edge of Canton. The vacant land, surrounded by residential housing, had been part of the recently defunct County Infirmary farm. If the college was willing to submit a minimum bid of $50,000 for the land, the county was willing to put up the property for sale at that price during an auction to be held in February 1956.

In the meantime, news of the school's relocation had been leaked to the local news media and United Press International. A delegation from Dover, Ohio, upon hearing of the pending move, asked the board to consider settling in the Dover-New Philadelphia area. Dover representatives even offered CBC officials $100,000 to help with moving expenses. In the end, the trustees chose Canton over a Dover location for three reasons: Canton, a much larger city than Dover, was without a college within its city limits, Canton was more centrally located to Friends churches, and the Canton property seemed especially suited for the college.

During another meeting in December 1955, the Board of Trustees voted to expand the Junior College program to a four-year liberal arts curriculum. As Osborne later recounted, "While the Bible College was rendering a most acceptable service to young people who desired to enter full time Christian service, it was not making provision for those who aspired to enter the teaching profession or other so-called secular vocations in life." In doing so, board members not only voted to approve the school's designation from a Bible to a liberal arts college, but concurrently honored its founders by renaming the school Malone College.

The Board's decision to transition to a liberal arts college modified the central focus of the Bible training school, Bible institute, and Bible college eras of the previous sixty-four years. Nevertheless,

Malone College never wavered from Walter and Emma Malone's original intent to provide sound Biblical teaching and practical experience for Christian service. Men and women enrolled at Malone College would still be trained for pastoral and other areas of Christian ministry, but hereafter students who chose different vocational paths could also be educated in a decidedly Christian setting at the Malones' school. The liberal arts chapter in the institution's history was about to commence, but the legacy of Walter and Emma Malone would be carefully preserved in the years to come.

Chapter 4: The Christian Liberal Arts College (1956–2008)

Malone College

It was a bitterly cold winter day on February 1, 1956, in Canton, Ohio. Despite the frigid temperatures, city and county officials, local developers, and curious bystanders gathered on the site of the old Stark County infirmary and farm. President Byron Osborne was among them. With $50,000 in hand, he planned to bid on two parcels of county-owned land that were part of the soon-to-be-closed infirmary. When the auction commenced, Dr. Osborne bid the full $50,000 on behalf of Malone College as he had promised local officials he would do the previous December.

This was a momentous occasion for the Canton community. Canton at the time was the largest city in the nation without its own college or university. Much to the dismay of many of the city's residents, an attempt to open a municipal college in the old Timken family mansion had failed at the ballot box in 1949. Since then, the desire for a local college remained undiminished, and representatives of Canton had vigorously lobbied Malone College administrators to relocate within the city's borders. So, when a second bid came in at $100,000

for those two parcels during the auction, President Osborne was not the only individual in the crowd who was disappointed. Canton officials were none too pleased themselves.

Dr. Osborne was at a loss. Now what? Although its Cleveland and Brecksville properties had recently been appraised at over $800,000, the college did not yet have those or any other funds at its disposal. In his 1970 history of the college, Osborne wrote, "That was a moment of tenseness for me. What could be done? How could one pay $100,000 in cash when only $50,000 was available? There was a moment of silent prayer, and just before the auctioneer was ready to let the property go to the bidder for $100,000, I said, '$101,000.' And so, the purchase was made by the College."

The Board of Trustees did secure the extra funds, although some faculty members were deeply troubled. Why had their earnest prayers gone unanswered? Why had the land cost over twice the amount for which the college had budgeted?

Fortunately, the story does not end there. Three years later, Malone College officials received word from the Ohio Highway Department that, yes, another freeway, what is now U.S. Route 62, would cross the college property near its northern border. After some haggling over the price, the government paid Malone College $86,525 for seven acres of its land. Thus, in the long run, the campus property had not been purchased for $101,000, but for $14,475.

But there was yet another sequel. Since a portion of the school's property was situated to the north of the new freeway on the south side of 30th Street NW, it was "orphaned" and could not be directly accessed from the main campus. Therefore, the Board approved a sale of the property and sold the 30th Street parcel for $40,000. In other words, the school came out ahead $25,525. Dr. Osborne rejoiced, "The Lord, in the words of the Apostle, had done exceeding, abundantly above all we had asked or thought." It was a rather auspicious beginning for Malone College in its new home in Canton, Ohio.

❧ ❧

I: A Christian Liberal Arts College: The Beginnings

The transition from a Bible college to a four-year liberal arts institution was momentous, but not unexpected. As early as 1898, the Malones added liberal arts classes to the school's course of study. In 1947, as already noted in the previous chapter, the trustees approved a junior college program by which students fulfilled their general education requirements at Cleveland Bible College before transferring to a college or university elsewhere. Given the success of the two-year junior college course and a desire for a more broad-based curriculum, the Board of Trustees had approved a motion on February 14, 1956, that Cleveland Bible College convert to a four-year liberal arts college.

Beyond the intrinsic value of immersing students in the arts and sciences, as well as theology, the newly-imagined Malone College offered even more. Board members and administrators aspired to offer a holistic and intentionally Christian education, foster spiritual and intellectual growth, cultivate wisdom, help students prayerfully intuit their calling, and prepare them for service both within their communities and vocationally. The 1957–58 catalog underscored this commitment: "The program of liberal arts education is developed and designed to introduce the student to a variety of fields of learning. Constant encouragement is given that he will gain wide knowledge and helpful skills in the search for truth and its application to his life and chosen vocation." The liberal arts curriculum was therefore designed "to promote the building of strong Christian character." Although some were concerned that the original mission of the school might be diluted or diminished, the Malone College community was focused on enhancing, rather than veering away from, Emma and Walter Malone's vision for a Christ-centered institution of higher learning.

The Malone College era was the longest in the school's history, lasting from 1956 to 2008. During this 52-year period, Malone College was situated in two cities and guided by seven presidents. The school grew from less than 300 students in 1956 to well over 2,000 by 2008. In time, a full complement of liberal arts and professional fields of study, degree-completion programs, and graduate degrees were added. The campus expanded via building construction and the donation or purchase of adjacent properties. Although Malone College did not start from "scratch," establishing a new liberal arts college was nevertheless a formidable task.

The initial challenge after the purchase of the Canton property was erecting campus structures on vacant farmland. Until its Cuyahoga County properties were sold, the school was cash poor. As college officials prepared to solicit construction bids for the new buildings, the institution had less than $5,000 on hand. Banks in Cleveland balked at extending loans for projects located outside of Cuyahoga County, and Canton banks had yet to establish a firm financial relationship with the college. The situation was so dire that one local Quaker offered to mortgage his home as a stopgap measure.

Lambert Huffman, the Malone trustee who facilitated the college's move to his hometown, was appointed as director of the building project and reached out to the business community for assistance. Canton native Luther Day, son of President William McKinley's Secretary of State and husband to Walter and Emma Malone's eldest daughter,

sought assistance "and acceptance" on behalf of the college from three of his friends: Paul Belden of the Belden Brick Company, William Umstattd of the Timken Company, and T. K. Harris of his eponymous real estate firm. With their imprimatur, local business leaders and vendors, representing a wide range of faiths—Catholic, Jewish, and Protestant—offered discounts on building supplies and equipment, donated funds and legal counsel, and extended grace on payment for services rendered. The community's largesse was nothing short of miraculous. Herman Grabowski's company took on the heating and plumbing contract when the college's coffers were still empty. Local businessman Marvin Mintz purchased the still unsold Euclid Avenue main campus so the college could pay for its upfront construction costs. When the Cleveland property was finally sold, the college reimbursed their benefactor. The Timken Foundation provided funding to help cover construction and endowment expenses for a science center in 1960 and donated twenty acres of land adjacent to Malone College. The football practice and soccer fields were later located on that parcel. Without these generous community leaders, as well as the financial support of the Evangelical Friends Church, the Malone story may well have ended during the school's sixty-fifth year. Instead, local folks began buzzing about the "Malone Miracle."

While a flurry of activity, such as fundraising, erecting new buildings, and selling the Cuyahoga County properties, was unfolding, the eleven members of the first Malone College graduating class, the Class of 1957, were receiving their

diplomas none too soon. Malone College administrators received notice from state and Cleveland officials that they must vacate the Esther Baird Residence Hall, which was situated on the future site of an expressway entrance ramp, by May 1957. President Osborne and his staff had little time to move an *entire college* from Cleveland to Canton by September 1957.

The relocation was not without its difficulties, so much so that some doubted the college would open in time for the start of the 1957–58 academic year. Lyle Strand, technical supervisor of the building project and later director of Malone's physical plant, remembered the frantic scramble to finish the structures by the first day of classes. Two weeks before opening day, President Osborne asked Strand if "we will make it." Fifty years later, Strand recalled, "I shall never know how or why I said, 'Oh, yes, Byron. We will make it.'"

On September 25, 1957, Malone College welcomed its students to the new campus on 25th Street Northwest in Canton. Two months later, all three of Walter and Emma Malone's daughters, Esther Malone Waterbury, Ruth Malone Osborne, and Margaret Malone Day, were on hand for the dedication of the school. Their brother, Walter J. Malone, Jr., a college president himself, was the featured speaker for the historic event.

Of course, some of the buildings were not quite ready for occupation when the students arrived. Since the construction team was still working on the nearly-finished women's dormitory, George Fox Hall, female residents could only inhabit their rooms after the dinner hour. Although the Main Building, now Founders Hall, was completed by the start of the academic year, the school still lacked a library, gymnasium, and residential housing for men on opening day. Male residents lodged at the Church of the Nazarene summer camp in nearby Louisville and at the Canton YMCA until Penn and Gurney Halls were erected. The inconveniences were temporary. By the mid-1960s, the college boasted a library, science building, gymnasium, physical plant, and several residence halls. Each of the residence halls was named in honor of an esteemed Quaker.

And so, Walter and Emma's school began its new chapter in Canton, Ohio. Although the college did not enjoy the same level of academic prestige as some of its sister Quaker colleges, much to the mild disappointment of some local citizens, Dr. Everett Cattell would later remark in his inaugural address in 1960, "Swarthmore and Haverford had their struggles, but in their struggling, there was strength." Malone too would be tested, he continued, but he had no doubt that the school would thrive.

In the meantime, President Osborne, administrators, faculty, and staff faced an ambitious undertaking as they guided the school's reconstitution as a Christian liberal arts college. The March 1959 issue of the *Malone Messenger* posed the question that the Malone community was pondering: "What type of institution does Malone College hope to become?"

To answer that question, Osborne drew upon the expertise and experience of talented Christian academics and administrators from other well-regarded schools, such as Wheaton College, Taylor University, and Winona Lake School of Theology, during the college's earliest phase of transition. In addition, many faculty wore multiple hats: they taught in the classroom while simultaneously shouldering administrative duties, whether as academic dean, divisional chair, registrar, or public relations director, to ensure the academic, financial, and spiritual stability of the college. Their principal goals during this "first period of establishment," as it was called, were to develop, finance, and fine-tune Malone's new educational programs.

One of the first matters college officials addressed was accreditation. Malone College remained a member of the Accrediting Association of Bible Institutes and Bible Colleges through 1957, but that relationship ended as Malone shifted to a liberal arts college. The regional accrediting agency for Midwestern colleges and universities, North Central Association of Colleges and Secondary Schools (NCA), advised President Osborne that the college could not begin the accreditation process until 1961. That was the year when the entering freshmen class of 1957 was scheduled to graduate. Under the dogged leadership of Dr. Roger Wood, the school crafted a comprehensive self-study, hosted a successful NCA team visit, and received notice of accreditation by NCA in 1964. Malone College's new status as a fully-accredited institution of higher learning raised the school's academic standing and attracted more students to the college.

How to commemorate this important, and crucial, achievement? The college sponsored a celebratory parade down the streets of Canton.

Accreditation was essential, but it could only be achieved if Malone College offered a solid and rigorous curriculum. Under the direction of Dr. Ronald Jones, the college's first chief academic officer, the faculty developed a wide array of

liberal arts majors. Malone College also offered professional courses of study in education and was affiliated with two vocational institutions, Aultman School of Nursing and Raedel Secretarial School. Students from these two organizations enrolled in some or all their classes on the Malone campus. The partnership with Aultman Hospital extended to a specialization in medical laboratory work. Medical Technology majors completed three years of coursework at Malone and one year at the Aultman Hospital School of Medical Technology. Students interested in engineering, medicine, and law prepared for these and other professional fields as well. Of course, the General

Education program, which was essential for grounding Malone College students in the liberal arts, was foundational. The first General Education curriculum was grouped into four main areas: Humanities, Religion, Science, and Social Sciences. Until the mid-1970s, students enrolled in two years of a foreign language, two laboratory science classes, and, if members of a Friends Church, a Quaker history course.

Another critical component in ensuring the long-term viability of Malone College was putting the school on solid financial footing. After securing funds and loans for the property and campus structures, the next hurdle college officials faced was securing $500,000 for an endowment fund as required by the State of Ohio for liberal arts colleges. With the help of Ohio Yearly Meeting (now Evangelical Friends Church: Eastern Region), which pledged $25,000 per year, and local donations, the state requirement was met. Even so, Osborne and Sam Kvasnica, an astute young man in his twenties when he was tapped as chief financial officer of the college, were careful about conserving limited resources.

Given the institution's dependence on tuition dollars, the exploding student population certainly helped. When Malone College first opened its doors in 1957, 267 students enrolled. Ten years later, the student population had more than quadrupled in size to 1,162. If there was any doubt that residents of Canton and its environs wanted a hometown college, the enrollment numbers offered clear validation.

With the school steadily growing in size, Dr. Osborne submitted a letter to the Board of Trustees informing its members that he planned to retire in June 1959. "I have seriously been questioning in my own mind," he wrote, "whether a man should continue in the office past the age of 65." Although Dr. Osborne officially continued as president for another year, he took a leave of absence in the fall of 1959, and newly-appointed Director of Public Relations Paul Uhrig served as Acting President until the end of Osborne's term.

After stepping down in 1960, Dr. Osborne and wife Ruth retired to their home nearby where he raised prize-winning poultry. A few of the trophies bestowed on his brightly-feathered chickens are housed in the Malone University archives. Dr. Osborne remained connected to the institution by publishing its first history in 1970 and serving as an officer of the Alumni Executive Board until his death in 1990.

The search for a new president began in earnest in the fall of 1959. Among the eight nominees, one candidate garnered the most support: Everett L. Cattell. However, Cattell was not interested in the position. Dr. Cattell, who received an honorary doctorate from Cleveland Bible College, had long been associated with the Malones' school and the Friends Church. Raised in a Quaker home in Alliance, Ohio, Cattell was appointed as adjunct professor of religious education and psychology at Cleveland Bible Institute while pastoring Cleveland First Friends Church in the early 1930s. In 1936, he and his wife Catherine DeVol Cattell, the daughter of Quaker medical missionaries, journeyed to India where they served on the mission field for twenty-one years. Upon their return in 1957, Dr. Cattell was appointed General Superintendent of Ohio Yearly Meeting and, by virtue of that position, was also a member of the Malone College Board of Trustees. He was busy enough.

Russell Meyers, Class of 1941 and a fellow trustee, prevailed upon Dr. Cattell to reconsider, and after a season of prayer and discernment, Cattell agreed to serve as Malone's seventh president. Everett Cattell, for whom the Malone College library was later named, was one of the longest-serving presidents in the school's history. Under his tenure, the college maintained an aggressive building program, revised its curricula offerings, and clarified its institutional identity.

With the self-study process completed under Dr. Cattell's watch, the 1965–66 college catalog announced that the school was about to embark on

a second phase of development. This period was characterized by an emphasis on securing more qualified professors, expanding course and major offerings, and enhancing the school's standing in the community. Yet, while the college valued the "intellectual arts," it remained Christian. Malone College's commitment to its religious heritage had not been abandoned in Canton.

II: "Christ's Kingdom First" and the Malone Experiment

In a letter to Dr. Osborne in March 1957, long-time Dean of Men, Amos Henry, posed several questions:

> What are to be the future standards of the College regarding dress [for] young women? What standards for physical education and sports attire are to be established? What requirements are to be enforced regarding the use of alcohol and tobacco, especially as it applies to dormitory students? Our move to Canton will undoubtedly project us into an area of closer scrutiny not only by Ohio Yearly Meeting but also by that portion of our local community which may not share our Christian views in particular matters.

These were critical questions. Cleveland Bible College students were expected to be devout evangelical Christians as they prepared for full-time or lay ministry. But what happens when the school is no longer a Bible college and admits students from the community who may not "agree with the position taken by the college?"

Without question, Malone College remained unshakably Christian. As the 1957–58 catalog pronounced, "Malone College is fully committed to the Christian ideal." The institutional seal, patterned after those at Harvard and Yale, reflected Malone's fidelity to the Christian faith. The school's motto, "*Regnum Christi Primum*" ("Christ's Kingdom First"), was drawn from Matthew 6:33.

Malone students could not help but notice that the college embodied its motto in tangible ways. Chapel was held daily on the second floor of Osborne Hall, and attendance was mandatory. Students enrolled in required Bible and theology courses and were expected to "live in harmony with the principles of conduct set forth in the Bible, thus to please and honor Jesus Christ." Faculty members were Christian, and most of them represented evangelical strands of their faith. Faculty, staff, administrators, and students were expected to abstain from the use of alcohol, tobacco, social dancing, and, until a theater program was established at Malone, "theater attendance." Residential students were required "to refrain from these at all times while under the jurisdiction of the college." All members of the community were "asked to constantly bear in mind that on campus or off we should represent Malone College in such a manner as to enhance its influence and reputation."

And yet, there was no longer a "religious test" for admission as had been the case before 1957. Instead, Malone College welcomed all students, regardless of their Christian commitment or lack thereof. The policy to admit nonbelievers and those who did not hail from an evangelical background came to be known as the *Malone Experiment*. The term can be traced back to a chapel address given by President Cattell in 1963. Simply put, the Malone Experiment provided an exemption for commuting students. Except when they were on campus grounds, nonresidential students, who administrators presumed lived with their families, were not subject to Malone's rules of conduct. Residential students, on the other hand, were required to abide by the school's regulations whether on or off campus. Needless to say, the "Malone Experiment" was not without its challenges. If nothing else, the school was applying a double

standard: one set of rules for residential students, who were required to abide by institutional regulations whether at Malone or not, and another for commuters, who were not similarly bound to Malone's code of social conduct when off campus. This became untenable.

In keeping with the traditional Quaker practice of consensus-seeking, President Cattell wrote an open letter to the Board of Trustees and faculty in 1966, asking for input in regards to Malone's conflicting policies for residential and commuting students. The president was not suggesting a change in on-campus regulations for either constituency, but rather a reconsideration of policies pertaining to off-campus deportment.

There were other factors at play in the debate as well. Nationwide, public universities were relinquishing their role as "temporary guardians" of their students, the legal relationship known as *in loco parentis*, as a result of judiciary decisions in several court cases. A number of private colleges and universities, both secular and religious, followed suit and eased out or eliminated institutional restrictions on student behavior. The national conversation about the "parental" role of the college did not go unnoticed by Malone students. By 1971, they were directly engaged in the debate over the school's rules and regulations that President Cattell had started in 1966. A campus survey revealed that a majority of students supported a modification of behavioral standards for residential students who ventured beyond the Malone College property.

After hearing competing voices from students, parents, faculty, staff, administrators, and trustees, President Cattell recommended to the Board of Trustees that Malone end off-campus oversight of student conduct. The Board of Trustees, in adopting the new policy, reminded the Malone community that "the behavior of Malone students and the maintenance of Malone ideals is a matter of sacred trust." Not all were pleased with the decision, and at least one faculty member resigned in protest. Even so, the episode was a testimony to the value of a collaborative decision-making process, in the manner of Friends, and the Malone community's genuine concern for the well-being of its students. Furthermore, the school's leadership team demonstrated that it welcomed disparate voices into the campus-wide conversations. Even though the solution was fraught with uncertainty, the institution's fundamental commitment to its Christian identity, its heritage, and its students was resolute.

Arts and Culture at Malone

Embedded within an informal understanding of the Malone Experiment was a desire to cultivate a closer relationship with local residents. With this in mind, the college fostered an enriched cultural and intellectual milieu that enhanced connections with inhabitants of Stark County and beyond. In 1965, President Cattell argued that as a Christian institution, Malone was committed to "open mindedness." That not only applied to good scholarship and teaching, but also to engagement with the larger community. To that end, Malone opened a concert and lecture series during the Cattell years. College administrators had been inviting special speakers to campus since Walter and Emma Malone were principals. However, the new series moved beyond exclusively religious themes and broadened Malone's artistic and intellectual influences.

In 1968, for example, the concert series featured performances by folk music group The

New Christy Minstrels, operatic bass talent Jerome Hines, the Cleveland Orchestra, Turnau Opera Players, and concert pianist Eugene Mancini. Lecture and chapel speakers included such figures as historian Timothy Smith, theologians D. Elton Trueblood and Carl F. H. Henry, Nazi concentration camp survivor Corrie Ten Boom, inspirational author Ann Kiemel Anderson, Ohio Governor John Gilligan, and United States Ambassador to the United Nations John Scali.

Although the Lyceum Series, as Malone's original concert and lecture series was known, eventually came to an end, the school maintained a full schedule of concerts and lectures throughout the Malone College era. Celebrate '78 brought Christian artists Randy Matthews, Petra, and Glad, among others, to campus. In 1999 Malone students and faculty founded the Worldview Forum. The purpose of the Worldview Forum, which is still held several times annually, was to provide opportunities "to practice critical thinking and civil dialogue in the comparison of various worldviews." The John Woolman Christian Scholar Lecture Series, named in honor of an eighteenth-century Quaker anti-slavery activist, was founded in 2008. The series brought leading Christian intellectuals to campus every spring. The diversity of the artists and speakers enriched the cultural life of the campus.

Malone College's own fine arts programs also enlivened the campus and surrounding community. Vocal music had been an integral component of the Bible institute curriculum since 1892. That rich heritage continued in the late 20th Century. The Malone College Chorale performed on campus and traveled throughout the United States, Central America, East Asia, Europe, and Africa over the years. In the 1960s and 1970s, community members annually joined the Malone chorale to perform Handel's *Messiah*. "He's Alive," an Easter cantata performed by the chorale in the 1970s and 1980s and the standing-room-only Christmas concerts throughout the Malone College era were especially popular. Women's Glee and Concert Choirs, a Chamber Choir, and student, faculty, and visiting artist recitals adorned the college's concert

schedule. As early as 1981, Chorale students sponsored a "Singing Valentines" fund-raiser every February. That popular tradition continues to the present day.

Instrumental music programs similarly enjoyed a long history at Malone College and its preceding institutions. Throughout the liberal arts college period, the school featured a concert band, several instrumental ensembles, and specialized training in piano and organ performance. As student enrollment increased substantially in the 1990s, brass choirs, woodwind ensembles, jazz bands, a piano preparatory program, and a marching band were added. In 1997, Professor Sandra Carnes produced the first "Grand Piano Extravaganza" at the Palace Theater in downtown Canton. In subsequent Grand Piano Extravaganza performances, as many as twenty-four faculty, student, and alumni pianists played on several grand pianos at once. Every year, the event packed the house.

Like Malone's music programs, the visual art program was founded during the Bible college years to provide students with another evangelistic tool. For most of the Malone College era, art majors were relegated to rather cramped quarters on the upper west side of Osborne Hall, but the surroundings did not impede the creative gifts of Malone students and faculty. Student artwork was displayed throughout the campus. As the art program grew, the Osborne location became problematic. In 2007, after the purchase and renovation of the Johnson Center for Worship and The Fine Arts, the visual art program moved to an enlarged and well-equipped area that featured several studios, classrooms, and galleries. The instrumental and vocal music programs were also relocated to the Johnson Center in 2007.

For much of the school's history, theater was considered a moral vice by a wide swath of evangelical Christians, including the Malones. In 1963,

that changed when a Dramatics Club was founded. Soon, the Malone Players were producing two major plays or musicals every year. One of the more innovative and favorite programs founded during

the Malone College era was the 24-Hour Theater. Within a 24-hour period, students held auditions, wrote five plays overnight, began practice the next morning, built the sets, and performed the newly-crafted plays to a studio audience. Similarly, the Ten-Minute Play Festival featured original plays. Malone students wrote, directed, acted, or designed sets. As many as twenty-five plays were performed over two nights.

In 2001, Professor Andrew Rudd launched the first student film festival. Later christened the Open Frame Film Festival, the annual one-night film fest featured the talents of student writers, producers, directors, and actors. Budding filmmakers approached their craft "from a faith-based perspective and [by] making films that tell all kinds of truth about human experience." Open Frame became so popular the event moved from the Johnson Center to the Palace Theater in downtown Canton to accommodate its growing viewing audience. These and other artistic forms of expressions reflected the ways in which Malone College cultivated all areas of student giftedness.

III: Education for 2000 A.D.

By the mid-1960s, Malone College had indeed become "Canton's college," and enrollment continued to grow. To accommodate an increasing student population and ever-expanding programs, the administration hired a record number of professors between 1967 and 1970. Adding to the school's academic prestige, an increasing proportion of faculty with earned doctorates were filling Malone's classrooms. To the delight of many, professors were leading students on intensive study trips to Europe every summer by the mid-1960s. A state-of-the art library was in the works, and the school catalog boasted about cutting-edge technology, such as movie, slide, overhead, and filmstrip projectors, tape recorders, and a 36-station modern language laboratory. While these technological enhancements may seem antiquated in hindsight, they helped ensure that the second phase of the school's development had been successful. Now, the college was ready to debut a "third" educational phase, known as "Education for 2000 A.D."

Education for 2000 A.D. was in part a response to the changing landscape in higher education. The State of Ohio invested heavily in public universities and vocational schools in the 1960s, drawing increasing numbers of students to state institutions.

Locally, Kent State University opened a branch campus just six miles north of Malone College in the fall of 1967. Two years later, Aultman Hospital School of Nursing transferred its students from Malone to the Kent State-Stark branch for their preliminary training. Even as Malone College was hiring dozens of new faculty members in the late 1960s, its student population was contracting. Enrollment dropped by over 25 percent within five years of the Kent-Stark branch opening.

Education 2000 A.D. was not only implemented to attract new students, but also to prepare them for the future. As the 1971–72 college catalog noted, Education for 2000 A. D. was "based on the realization that the graduate of the 1970s will be at the height of his contribution and influence in 2000 A. D. Therefore, the college must prepare the student not only for the '70s but for the 21st century as well." The new program, which essentially provided a General Education template at Malone College for the next thirty-five years, emphasized critical and creative thinking, the sciences, and computer skills. Malone was among the first colleges in the area to offer a course on

computer literacy and programming as part of its General Education requirements. In addition, a senior capstone course, "God, the World, and Man," was added to help students "pull together in a Christian context" their overall college experience. The new General Education package focused on preparing Christian leaders for all areas of endeavor and promoted the value of lifelong learning.

As part of the Education for 2000 A.D. plan, Malone College changed from a semester to a term system in 1970. The academic year was comprised of three terms, each nine-and-a-half weeks in length, and a three-week December Term. Students enrolled in just one course during December Term, during which freshmen and sophomores engaged in either a study of a contemporary issue, such the environment, or a non-Western culture on an alternative-year basis. Juniors had the opportunity to conduct an independent project, and seniors enrolled in "God, the World, and Man." December Term also presented various off-campus experiences as well. Some students spent December Term on the ski slopes of Colorado, while biology majors traversed the jungles of Central America to study tropical flora and fauna. Students who enrolled in the Human Awareness Program (HAP), established in 1972 by Dr. James Stuckey, lived in central Cleveland, sojourned to an Appalachian community in Kentucky, dwelled among the Cherokee in North Carolina, or served at missions in Mexico and

Guatemala during consecutive December Terms throughout the 1970s. A precursor to both the current service-learning program and the Social Work major, HAP offered more than December Term trips. During fall, winter, and spring terms, HAP included introductory courses and field internships for students concerned about the economically and socially disadvantaged in Canton and Stark County. These and other Education for 2000 A.D. courses, according to the 1972–74 college catalog, reinforced the school's commitment to "integrate the whole into a worldview consistent with the Christian faith."

55

Education 2000 A.D. was not limited to the classroom. Chapel remained a central component of the Malone experience, but by this time it was held three times per week instead of five. The place of worship changed too. Chapel services were relocated to Bethel Temple, situated just to the west of campus, and the old chapel location on the upper east level of Osborne was transformed into the Student Union. A snack bar, pinball machines,

pool tables, student mailboxes, and the Student Senate office, which doubled as a used bookstore, drew students to the Student Union, and Osborne Hall became their central gathering place.

The third phase of educational development at Malone College also addressed limited classroom and library space. By the end of 1971, a new library building was finally completed, and students were asked to assist in moving 62,000 volumes from the Main Building to the new location. Rain prevented the transfer of library materials on the scheduled day, reported *The Aviso* in December 1971, and far fewer students volunteered the following day to carry the materials to their new home. In a brilliant move to compel the students help with the transfer of materials, reported *The Aviso*, the cafeteria staff postponed dinner until the last books were placed in their new home. The theater program, which had been using Osborne Hall

for its productions, moved into the old library, where it presently remains. Fittingly, the new library was named in honor of Malone's outgoing president, Everett Cattell. Shortly after the library opened, President Everett Cattell, after twelve years in office, retired at the end of the 1971–72 academic year. After retiring, he published two books on Christian mission and theology and traveled with his wife and the Malone University Chorale to Taiwan, where their daughter her family served as missionaries, in 1974.

IV: Challenges and Opportunities

Dr. Cattell's successor, Lon D. Randall, was one of the youngest presidents in the history of Malone, but he came with a wealth of experience in international affairs and Christian higher education. Although not a Friend, he earned his undergraduate degree from a sister

Bible college and shared a "holiness" theological heritage similar to that of the Malones. Malone College would need his expertise as it navigated the unsettled waters of the 1970s. Enrollment figures stabilized at around 850 students during most of Randall's tenure, but the significant drop in Malone's student population after Kent State University opened its local branch left the college in financial distress by the time Dr. Randall was appointed in 1972. Although the Randall administration balanced the budget for eight years in a row, financial stability came at a heavy price. In time, the French, German, Spanish, and speech programs were eliminated, faculty were laid off, and publications and other expenses were sharply curtailed. An inflationary cycle coupled with a recession nationally also taxed the management skills of the new president.

Despite the budgetary pitfalls, the college persevered, adjusted to new fiscal realities, and refined its outreach efforts. School officials adopted a new motto, "A College of Persons," and a new logo. In response, some students playfully referred to their school as "The College of Dots." Several

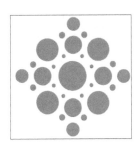

new programs were added, including Communication Arts, Computer Science, and Social Work majors, and Allied Health tracks in Certified Registered Nurse Anesthetist and Radiological Science. Malone College also hosted several academic conferences in the 1970s, such as the Midwest Writers Conference, the Christianity and Literature Conference, and the Conference on Faith and History.

Additionally, the Weaver Child Development Center opened in the old health center, an Associate of Arts in Early Childhood Education offered new vocational opportunities, scholarships for international students increased ethnic diversity on campus, and an exchange program between Malone College and Hong Kong Baptist University established in 1977 enabled Malone faculty to acquire international teaching experience. Dr. James Stanley, professor of political science, was the first of several Malone faculty who served as visiting professors in Hong Kong. The Coalition of Christian Colleges and Universities, under the direction of future Malone College President Gordon Werkema, inaugurated its first off-campus study semester, the American Studies Program (ASP), in 1976. During Winter Term 1977, Gordon Martin, Class of 1978, became the first Malone student to participate in ASP in Washington, DC. Martin's three daughters and two of his sons-in-law would later graduate from his alma mater.

The Randall era also marked the first time that Malone students enjoyed their own designated campus center. Plans for a newly-constructed student union had long been in the works, but when Canton City School District sold part of its Cleveland Avenue property to Malone College in 1976, a new opportunity arose. The recently-acquired property included an old barn that had been part of the county infirmary and farm complex. President Randall asked the college's architectural firm to conduct a feasibility study on the barn. Originally constructed in 1923, the barn was completed renovated and eventually housed student mailboxes, a café, a gaming room, lounges, a prayer chapel, offices for student clubs and Student Development, and, for a short period of time, chapel services. By the beginning of the 1977–78 academic year, the campus center was fully refurbished and ready to welcome Malone students. The building was eventually christened

Randall Campus Center, and it continues to serve as a campus hub.

Like his predecessor, Dr. Randall was committed to cultivating ties with local residents and was particularly adept at reaching out to the Canton community. After the Board of Trustees approved a three-year plan to eliminate the school's deficit in 1972, Randall and his team secured a significant contribution from the Timken Educational and Charitable Trust to help reduce operational debt. President Randall actively fostered partnerships between Malone and its Advisory Council and Women's Advisory Council. Members of both organizations offered wise suggestions and generous gifts to Malone College.

Another avenue through which the college connected with the community during the Randall years was the Malone Athletic Club. The athletic club was established to encourage parents of student-athletes and friends of the college to support the school's various sports teams. The membership fee was $5.00 per person. The founding of the new club was timely. Not only was Dr. Randall a strong supporter of Malone athletics, but he witnessed firsthand the fruition of a decade-long effort by the Athletics Department to establish a premier sports program at Malone.

Athletics at Malone

As already recounted, Walter and Emma Malone added "physical culture" classes to the curriculum shortly after they founded their Bible institute. By the time Malone opened its doors in Canton, the intramural program had been in existence for nearly twenty years. However, the Malones' school had yet to field an intercollegiate athletic team. Little did colleges administrators in 1957 know that by the end of Malone's membership in the National Association of Intercollegiate Athletics (NAIA) in 2011, the athletics program would produce over 400 NAIA All-Americans, 26 individual NAIA national champions, cross country and golf NAIA national championship teams, several more National Christian College Athletic Association (NCCAA) national title teams, and countless district, regional, and conference titles and national championship appearances.

The first intercollegiate sport introduced at Malone College began rather inauspiciously. The men's basketball team was established during the school's first year in Canton. Charles Bancroft, Class of 1952, was appointed to be the first coach of the team. Because Osborne Hall had not yet been constructed, the team practiced three days per week at the local YMCA and Jewish Community Center. The men competed against junior varsity teams from across Indiana and Ohio and finished its first season with a respectable 5–7 win-loss record.

The basketball team was known as the "Big Red" until the Pioneer mascot was selected in the fall of 1959. In keeping with the school's tradition of consensus, several students suggested the name, which then was approved by student council and the faculty. Chemistry professor and administrator Donald Starr later reminisced that the name "Pioneers" was in keeping with the challenging "journey" from Cleveland to Canton. The school colors were red and white. A third color, dark blue, was added in the mid-1970s. Inspired by the moose head, which hovered over students in Timken Science Hall and later Randall Campus Center, Malone introduced its spirit character, Maxamoose, in 2002.

With the opening of Walsh College less than five miles away in 1960, Malone found its sports rival. And a spirited rivalry it was. The Mayor's Cup basketball game was initially played during the 1964–65 season. Walsh College won the first game in 1965, but Malone won the following year and was the first to retire a Mayor's Cup, which required three consecutive Mayor's Cup victories, in 1971. When the City of North Canton later

extended its borders to include the Walsh campus, the annual competition became known as the Mayors' Cup.

In 1960, the athletics department introduced its second team sport: wrestling. However, wrestling never moved beyond club status and was dropped after the initial year. In the early 1970s, several Malone students from wrestling powerhouse Euclid High School, located a few miles from the old CBC campus, convinced Millard Niver, a math professor, to coach a wrestling team. Although Dr. Niver was new to the sport, he agreed and wrestling reappeared on campus in 1971. The program produced three NAIA All-Americans before being disbanded a second time in 1986.

The men's track, men's cross country, golf, tennis, baseball, and soccer teams were added in quick succession by the mid-1960s. Perhaps the most momentous event in all of Malone sports' history took place in 1967 when Jack Hazen was appointed as a professor of physical education and coach of the cross country and track teams. Coach Hazen's first cross country team posted a win-loss record of 2 and 9, hardly indicative of the successes yet to come. A mere five years later, Hazen's runners brought home Malone's first national team

Jack Hazen: Fifty Years at Malone

Few coaches have as storied a career as Jack Hazen, who arrived at Malone as Assistant Professor of Physical Education and coach of the cross country and track teams in 1967. Hazen has served as head coach of men's cross country at Malone University for over 50 years and as women's cross country head coach for 26 years. His men's program still ranks as the all-time winningest program by the NAIA, and his 1972 men's team became the first Malone team to earn an NAIA national championship, while his 1999 women's team became the second.

The Pioneers captured a total of four men's cross country national titles and one women's cross country title during Hazen's tenure. Malone's rich tradition of cross country success continued throughout the institution's transition to NCAA Division II membership. In 2014, the women's team became the first NCAA Division II program to claim the All-Ohio Championship, one of only two non-Division I programs to capture the overall All-Ohio Title. On the men's side, Malone claimed eight overall All-Ohio Championships, the last one coming in 2008.

Hazen also served as the head coach of men's track and field for 28 years and women's track and field for three years. He has coached over 325 NAIA All-Americans in cross country and track & field, which represents over 80% of the All-Americans in Malone athletics history.

Coach Hazen served as an assistant for the USA Track and Field Team during the 2012 Olympic Games and coached at several other international meets. In 2016, Hazen received the Lifetime Achievement Award from the Ohio Association of Track and Cross Country Coaches (OATCCC) for 100 total seasons of coaching service. In 2017, Coach Hazen was elected into the Coaches Hall of Fame of the U.S. Track & Field and Cross Country Coaches Association.

Most importantly, Hazen continues to invest in student-athletes and impact their lives for Christ at Malone University.

Mark Bankert,
Assistant Professor of Sports Management

title when they won the NAIA national championship in 1972. Hazen not only coached Malone athletes, but his brilliance as mentor and trainer brought him coaching stints at the national and international levels.

Malone's first individual national champion, however, was a golfer, Ken Hyland, Class of 1969. The golf team's fortunes improved markedly when Hyland joined the team as a freshman. He went on to win conference and district honors, as well as the national title, over the next four years. Hyland returned to Malone in 1973 as coach of the men's golf team and has successfully served in that capacity since then. Hyland coached the NAIA national championship golf team in 2000 and the NAIA individual national champion in 2010.

The last of the men's sports teams founded in the Malone College era was the football team. College administrators discussed fielding an intercollegiate football team as early as 1958, but it wasn't until 1993 that a football program was established. A year later, the Pioneer Spirit Marching Band was founded. Comprised of musicians, field commanders, majorettes, and a color guard, the Pioneer Spirit Marching Band has provided half-time entertainment at Malone football home games since 1994.

All the men's teams enjoyed their moments of glory, each making at least one appearance at nationals. The men's basketball team participated in three national championship series, the baseball team appeared in the NAIA World Series in 1973 and won the NCCAA World Series National Championship in 2006, the men's cross-country team won three consecutive national championships between 2007 and 2009, the men's tennis team appeared at three nationals, and the football team captured the national title at the NCCAA Victory Bowl in 2007. Even more importantly, 401 Malone male and female athletes were recognized

as All-America Scholar Athletes while the school was a member of NAIA. Baseball player Scott Thomson, Class of 1979, was the first Malone scholar-athlete to be recognized. Four years later, volleyball player Lori Blyer, Class of 1985, was Malone's first female NAIA All-America Scholar Athlete.

In keeping with prevailing gender mores that tended to marginalize women in sports, the school did not field a women's team during Malone's first decade in Canton. This, of course, was not unusual for the period. However, a cheerleading squad

was formed in 1958. Throughout the college era, Malone cheerleaders enthusiastically rooted for the men's basketball, soccer, wrestling, and football teams. The first male cheerleader, Dusty Rhodes, appears in the 1962 *Philos* yearbook. Male cheerleaders did not reappear until the 1980s and only periodically joined Malone squads thereafter.

Finally, in 1967, Malone College established a women's basketball team, the first female intercollegiate sports team in the school's history. The women's basketball program, which later appeared in two national tournaments, also produced the school's first female All-American, Gloria Blanks, Class of 1984, during the 1981–82 season. After the women's basketball program was organized in 1967, eight years passed before a second women's intercollegiate athletic program was fielded. In fact, two more sports teams were added during the 1975–76 season, volleyball and women's tennis. The passage of Title IX of the Education

Amendments of 1972, which mandated that "no person in the United States shall, on the basis of sex, be excluded from participation in…any education program or activity receiving Federal financial assistance," prompted Malone College, as well as other institutions of higher learning across the country, to ensure that college women had a wider range of intercollegiate sports opportunities.

By 2000, Malone was fielding women's track and field, cross country, softball, soccer, and golf teams. Monica Stevenson became Malone's first female NAIA national champion by winning the 600-yard individual race in 1990. Other women's programs also flourished. Each of the women's teams made at least one AIAW (Association for Intercollegiate Athletics for Women), NAIA, or NCCAA national tournament appearance during the Malone College era. Female sports teams won national championships too. The women's cross-country team won the NAIA national championship title in 1999, and the women's soccer team brought home the NCCAA national championship trophy in 2002. Female, as well as male, athletes burnished Malone's growing reputation for sports excellence.

In time, several of these athletes received special recognition from the college. In 1985, Malone's longtime baseball coach and Athletic Director Bob Starcher partnered with the Alumni Executive Board to establish the Malone College

Athletics Hall of Fame. Members of the first class to be inducted were David Fross, '68, Ken Hyland, '69 and William Scholl, '73. Inductees were graduates of Malone or coaches with at least ten years of service "who distinguished themselves in athletics." Since its founding, over one hundred Malone College and Malone University coaches and alumni athletes have been inducted in the Athletics Hall of Fame. The Hall of Fame is the singular most meaningful way in which Malone acknowledges not only the athletic talents of its alumni, but also their academic, vocational, and service gifts and contributions as well.

Regardless of each team's win-loss record, the Athletics Department focused on living out

the school's motto: Christ's Kingdom First. The coaching staff during the Malone College era was "Christ-centered in their approach and fostered excellence in the classroom and on the field, court, greens, and track." Coaches and student-athletes lived out their mission in several ways. After four area basketball coaches, including Malone's veteran coach Hal Smith, were diagnosed with a rare liver disease, Malone co-sponsored the annual Hoops 4 Healing Tournament and other local events for fifteen years to raise money to combat liver disease. Student-athletes volunteered in after-school programs, assisted relief agencies during local emergencies, collected goods for the impoverished, and lent a helping hand for campus service events. The mission of each sports program was, and still is, to "glorify God."

V: Renewing the Vision

In May 1981, Dr. Randall was appointed associate director of the Peace Corps and resigned from his position at Malone. Randall had guided the school back to economic health and institutional stability by the mid-1970s, but a deepening recession and an inflationary cycle contributed to a fourteen percent downturn in student enrollment by the end of Randall's tenure. Student population dropped from 896 students in 1976 to 770 in 1981. Malone College was not alone during this crisis. In 1978, nearly every private college and university in Ohio reported a decline in enrollment. With the loss of a dynamic leader and yet another financial crunch, Malone's future seemed uncertain.

In September 1981, the Malone College Board of Trustees appointed a new president, Dr. Gordon R. Werkema. Like his predecessor, Werkema was an experienced administrator in Christian higher education. Before coming to Malone, he had served as president or chief academic officer at three Christian colleges and had been appointed in 1975 as the first president of what is now the Coalition of Christian Colleges and Universities. Werkema's first year as president at Malone College would not be an easy one. He faced enrollment and budget woes similar to those of the early 1970s.

Fortunately for Werkema, a promising constellation of people and events coalesced during the first few years of his administration. In 1981, Werkema appointed Dr. Ronald G. Johnson as chief academic officer of Malone College. A former student at Malone, Johnson had served as a physics professor at the school during the previous decade. A specialist in radiation biophysics,

 Dr. Johnson spent a brief period in the health sector before the new president convinced him to return to Malone. With his deep roots in the Friends tradition, his personal faith commitment, and his scholarship and teaching experience, Johnson proved to be a valuable partner for Werkema and a key reason for the school's rejuvenation over the next quarter of a century. Even more so than in the recent past, both Werkema and Johnson were also keen on guiding the institution toward a more intentionally Christian focus. Administrators replaced the "College of Persons" motto and seal with the original "Christ's Kingdom First."

Of course, the nation's economic recovery contributed to Malone's return to financial health as students began to enroll in higher numbers. Within one year of Werkema's arrival, enrollment jumped over thirteen percent. Enrollment continued to climb steadily, and by the fall of 1985, the student population had grown by 35 percent over four years. In 1985, for the first time since Fall Semester 1968, Malone's student population numbered over one thousand.

The jump in enrollment was in part attributed to Malone's renewed focus on its Christian heritage, the dedication of the admissions staff and the extended Malone community, and the founding of the Malone College Management Program (MCMP) in 1984. Under the direction of long-time professor Donald R. Murray, MCMP was an accelerated degree-completion program, one of the first of its kind in the nation, which enabled non-traditional students to complete a baccalaureate degree in management in fourteen months.

Several Malone faculty representing a variety of disciplines initially served as the primary instructors for each MCMP cohort. Eventually, dedicated MCMP faculty positions for the program were added. In 1985, 125 students were enrolled in the MCMP program, and ten years later, nearly forty percent of the entire Malone College graduating class was MCMP majors. Traditional and non-traditional enrollment continued to increase. In 1987, the student population surpassed the 1,200-mark for the first time in the school's history.

Malone College also expanded other undergraduate offerings during Werkema's tenure. In 1987, the college established its own nursing program. The Spanish major was reinstated the following year. To accommodate the additional programs, Werkema proposed a reorganization in which the number of academic departments expanded from six to thirteen. The "Word of the King" radio program had been defunct since the end of the Osborne administration, but the school established WMAL, Malone's own radio station, in 1981. At the time, it was the only contemporary Christian music radio station in the area.

As the school expanded in size, so too did the number of faculty, administrators, and support staff who were employed at Malone College. With the larger numbers of faculty and administrators, casual conversations in the hallway, monthly faculty business meetings, or yearly faculty retreats were becoming less effective than they had once been in addressing increasingly complex matters of governance, curricula, or promotion and tenure. As a result, the first Faculty Senate was organized during the Werkema years. Comprised of nine senators and a chair, Faculty Senate still serves as the collective voice of Malone's faculty. In time, Malone staff members formed their own organization, Staff Fellowship. Led by an elected president and committee members, Staff Fellowship offered a time of communal prayer, devotion, and fellowship. Although Staff Fellowship went moribund in the early 2010s, staff members continue to gather together biannually and often more frequently.

Perhaps the most important legacy of the 1980s was the administration's emphasis on the "integration of faith, learning, and living" within and beyond the classroom. Werkema not only focused on recruiting students with higher ACT and SAT scores, but also those from Christian secondary schools. Christian scholars were invited to campus to speak on the integration of faith and learning, and professors were awarded stipends to attend lectures and workshops on Christianity and higher education. The integration of faith and learning became a hallmark of a Malone College education.

Faith, Learning, and Living: Christian Ministry & Service at Malone

Although a focus on the institution's Christian heritage waxed and waned ever so slightly during the college era, it was never abandoned and remained central throughout every one of the seven presidential administrations between 1956 and 2008. Before graduating, students were still required to enroll in two Bible classes (Old and New Testament) and a senior capstone course that explored the Christian faith. Although the number of weekly chapel services was reduced from five to two between 1956 and 1977, chapel remained a staple of campus life throughout the Malone College years.

An essential component

in nurturing students' spiritual well-being was the relationship between students and their professors, coaches, and residential staff. Students and alumni shared both anecdotally and on standardized surveys their appreciation for Malone College faculty. Professors frequently invited students into their homes as part of orientation activities, as College Experience instructors, as progressive dinner hosts, or as residence hall "parents." Faculty and staff served as club and class advisors, judges and participants for Student Activities Council events, and Bible study leaders. They listened to, prayed with, and kept their office doors open for their students.

Coaches mentored student-athletes on the field and off. A number of alumni went on to serve in sports ministries after graduation, as directors of sports programs in local churches, or as athletes and administrators in such organizations as Athletics in Action. Some returned to Malone College to coach. Similarly, Student Development

staff and resident assistants cared deeply about the spiritual well-being of their charges. They too led Bible studies, prayed with students, and offered an encouraging word to residents and commuters. The Student Development Office also hosted a counseling center, which was established to provide professional Christian counseling. The spiritual welfare of Malone College students remained paramount.

In addition to regular chapel services, Malone College offered a range of other opportunities for spiritual growth. Annual Founders Week, Missions Week, Spiritual Emphasis Week, and Missions Conferences featured Christian scholars, musicians, missionaries, and evangelists. The yearly Youth Conference provided spiritual enrichment for high schoolers and served as a recruiting tool for the admissions team. As already noted, the first Youth Conference was hosted by the Cleveland Bible College Gleaners Club in 1941. Youth Conferences continued to be held at Malone College through the 1972–73 academic year. In the early 1980s, Malone students began attending the Jubilee Conference, sponsored by the Coalition for Christian Outreach, every February in Pittsburgh. It was one of many ways in which the college fostered spiritual development among its students.

Although Malone College continued to train future pastors and missionaries as it had in Cleveland, the school was without a campus minister for much of the college era. The first chaplain at Malone College, James Reapsome, was appointed in 1967. Reapsome's tenure was brief,

and the position largely remained vacant until Randy Heckert was appointed as campus pastor in 1997. Malone alumna Linda Leon, Class of 1993, was installed as Director of Campus Ministries. These hires marked the first time since the school's arrival in Canton that significant resources had been dedicated to campus ministries. The Campus Ministries team, which also included part-time and volunteer staff, coordinated chapel programs, student participation in Jubilee, Bible studies, service-learning trips, and other areas of Christian service.

Even before the Campus Ministries Office was organized, student-led organizations continued to focus on service and evangelism. Their activities embodied a long tradition of Christian service that began with Walter and Emma Malone. The Missionary League, a holdover from the Cleveland Bible College days, supported missionaries Jim and Doris Morris, Ella Ruth Pratt, and Norma Freer, all CBC graduates, well into the 1960s. The long-standing Soul Winners Club was soon replaced by the Varsity Ambassadors organization. This club held an annual Inter-Varsity Conference

during the first decade in Canton. The Christian Service Club first appeared in 1960. In 1962, members of the club visited inmates at the Stark County Jail, children at the local juvenile detention center, and the elderly at the county nursing home. Near the end of the Malone College era, students concerned about human trafficking joined alumni, faculty, and Campus Ministries staff in founding a new social justice organization. Coined "be:Justice" by Joel Daniel Harris '04, the club sponsored activities to heighten campus awareness about a wide range of social ills and raised funds for local social welfare organizations. In these and a myriad of other ways, the Malone community ensured that the institution's commitment to Christian stewardship, service, and evangelism was not abandoned when the school moved to Canton.

Additionally, Malone students participated in several national and local philanthropic events and partnered with a variety of social service agencies. For example, on April 22, 1970, Malone students marked the first annual Earth Day by collecting over 800 pounds of trash along U.S. Route 62 between Cleveland and Market Avenues. Students then placed some of the refuse and several mementos in a coffin and buried the waste-filled casket near the Main Building. The coffin remains in place to this day near Founder's Hall as a poignant reminder of the importance of Creation care.

In partnership with the Stark County Hunger Task Force, Malone students began participating in a "gleaning project" in 1985. Inspired by the Biblical example of Ruth, students gathered

produce from already-harvested fields at area farms every October for nearly a decade and donated their gleanings to the local food bank. In the 1980s and 1990s, Malone sponsored its own Habitat for Humanity student chapter, and its members helped construct housing for Stark County and Appalachian-area families. Love the Children Ministries (LCM) was founded by Malone freshman Heather Conley Craig '08 in December 2004. The organization hosted a Christmas party and provided presents for children of the working poor. LCM's first Christmas party served 90 children. Assisted by Malone students, alumni, and friends over the years, LCM was serving over 300 children annually by 2015. Malone students also volunteered with Big Brothers Big Sisters of America, the YMCA, the YWCA, emergency shelters, animal shelters, health clinics, local parks, and other service agencies. They raised funds for or personally ministered to disaster victims, the poor, the homeless, the marginalized, and the sick. They also cared for their own; that is, they gave of themselves to students, faculty, staff, alumni, and members of the extended Malone family who found themselves in crisis.

Students expressed their faith in joyful worship as well as service. In the late 1980s, several students founded the forerunner of what is now known as "Celebration." First known as "Thursdays: The Encounter Hour Bible Study," the weekly student-led worship service was held in the Randall Campus Center's Bennett Lounge at 9:00 p.m. every Thursday. By 1990 the worship service was simply called "Thursdays," and, in 1994, Thursdays was renamed "Crossfire." The following

year, participants finally settled on the name "Celebration." Still student-run, Celebration met every other Thursday for "worship and fellowship hour" in Randall Campus Center. By 2000, between three and four hundred students were attending Celebration every other week. Although the venue changed to the Johnson Center by the end of the Malone College era, students still gather for prayer, Bible study, and worship every other Thursday for Celebration.

As their CBI and CBC predecessors had done before them, Malone students took their spiritual and creative gifts on the road. A wide array of Christian outreach groups performed at churches, camp meetings, and revival services. During the school's first decade in Canton, Malone sponsored several vocal ministry groups, many with names reminiscent of the girl groups and boy bands of the early 1960s: Canaanaires Quartet, King's Messengers, Harmony-Aires, Melody-Aires, Crusaders, and Chantonettes. Traveling groups during the Randall administration included The

Sonshine Company, Boanerges, and Naphtali, among others. Still Water, which featured the musical talents of Malone students from 1981 to 1983, was followed by Potter's Clay in 1983. Successive editions of Potter's Clay performed at a variety of venues across the country, including Disney World, until 1988. Future "Over the Rhine" vocalist Karin Bergquist '88 was a member of one of the later versions of Potter's Clay. Just as Potter's Clay was disbanding, His Faithful Servants formed. Founded in 1988, His Faithful Servants was one of the longest-lasting vocal groups in the school's history. The group represented Malone College as ambassadors in Christian outreach until the early 2000s.

Traveling teams not only displayed the vocal and instrumental talents of Malone College students. The Chancel Players performed Christian comedy and drama acts and, like its musical counterparts, traveled extensively on behalf of the college. The troupe endured even longer than His Faithful Servants. The ministry team was founded in 1972 and, despite a few gaps over the years, was still performing as the school celebrated its 125th anniversary in 2017. Other outreach groups included a three-member clown team that performed from 1977 to 1979, and Acts of Faith, a mime troupe that performed from late 1990s to the mid-2000s.

Not all traveling groups were performers. The annual European summer trips in the 1960s, the Human Awareness Program immersion experiences of the 1970s, and the mission trips of the 1980s eventually gave way to the service-learning program in the 1990s. Faculty and staff led students on one- to four-week trips to Austria, China, Costa Rica, Ecuador, India, Italy, Kenya, Poland, Thailand and other faraway places to learn about the culture, faith, history, and people living outside of the United States. Domestic student-learning

trips to downtown Canton, Pine Ridge Indian Reservation, and Chicago were no less valuable. Service was a central component of the trips. Students served lunch to homeless refugees in Italy, sorted and packed donated items for disaster victims in Hong Kong, conducted health clinics in Haiti, or partnered with a city mission in Germany. During these and other Malone trips, students came away with a greater appreciation for the multitudinous ways of living and learning in other societies and a developed a deeper understanding about the intrinsic value of people and cultures very different from their own.

VI: Building for the Future

In March 1989, the Board of Trustees announced the appointment of E. Arthur "Woody" Self as the new president of Malone College. President Werkema had resigned six months earlier, and Vice

President Ronald Johnson was serving as interim president. Dr. Self arrived with wide-ranging experiences in higher education as both a professor and administrator at number of colleges and universities, including Friends University, a sister Quaker institution. Although Self's tenure was merely five years in length, he transformed the physical landscape of the institution, hosted Malone College's centennial celebration, oversaw an explosive growth in student enrollment, and inaugurated Malone's first graduate program.

Within a year of President Self's arrival, he drafted an aggressive building scheme. By 1990, plans were underway for a new dining hall and residential buildings. Construction on College Hill, now DeVol Hall, commenced in 1991 and was dedicated in January 1992. Although College Hill was designed to accommodate married couples, it primarily housed single female students for twenty years before becoming a men's residence hall. The first level of the building also provided much-needed classroom space. Raising funds for the Brehme Centennial Center, which eventually housed the dining hall, mail room, bookstore, and classrooms, was slower going. Funds were finally secured for the completion

of Brehme Centennial Center, and the building opened in January 1994. However, plans for a conference center on the north side of the building did not come to completion for another decade. In the meantime, another residential facility, Heritage Hall, was constructed for men. During this flurry of campus construction, classrooms were added to Strand Physical Plant, Founders Hall (formerly the Main Building) underwent renovations, Hoover Courtyard was erected, and a new Alumni Gateway welcomed members of the Malone community and visitors to campus.

Until College Hill was christened in 1992, every other Malone College residence hall had been named in honor of a Quaker luminary. Of course, both Presidents Osborne and Cattell, who oversaw the construction of the existing dormitories on campus, were born and bred as Friends. President Self was not. However, the names bestowed on Heritage Hall and Brehme Centennial Center did pay homage to the founders, if indirectly. In 1992, Malone College marked the one hundredth year since its founding, and the naming of the dining and residence halls recognized that feat. The expansive building program, as well as a new logo that featured a torch, reflected the college's gratitude to Emma and Walter Malone.

The institution's centennial celebration was not the only impetus for new construction. Malone's student population was growing. As it had in the 1980s, Malone College mirrored a national trend.

High school graduates across the nation were attending colleges and universities in ever-larger numbers. However, while the number of students attending college increased six percent nationally during the Self years, Malone's student body exploded in numbers by comparison. It grew by an astonishing thirty-seven percent between 1989 and 1994.

Part of this increase was due to the addition of new programs and opportunities for students. Under the direction of Dr. Marcia Everett, a revised first-year experience program was added to the General Education curriculum for traditional freshmen students in 1992. The newly-established College Experience class, now in its third decade, not only helped students navigate their first semester in college, but also bolstered retention rates. Freshmen students met their College Experience instructors and peer leaders, known as Course Assistants, during Orientation Week. On the following two days, each College Experience section traveled to Camp Gideon in the rolling hills of east central Ohio to partake in a day of community-building activities or instead volunteered "Into the Streets" at local non-profit service agencies throughout Stark County. The centerpiece of Malone's first-year program was, and continues to be, the College Experience seminar. Instructors and peer mentors met weekly with freshmen students during Fall Semester. Topics were framed by key questions related to vocational exploration,

calling, faith, community, intellectual growth, and academic persistence. First-year students were, and still are, welcomed by and initiated into this intentional learning community from the moment they arrived on campus.

Other new programs were inaugurated during the Self years. As early as 1988, school administrators began to lay the groundwork for a grad-

uate program in education. In 1989, the Ohio Board of Regents approved Malone's petition to offer the Master of Arts in Education degree with core tracks in Reading or Curriculum and Instruction. The first graduate classes were offered during summer sessions in 1990. Communication Arts was added to the growing array of undergraduate majors. Off-campus study opportunities through the Coalition of Christian Colleges and Universities or Malone's own Guatemala Teacher Education and Costa Rica Tropical Ecology programs enriched students' intellectual growth and vocational preparation. Other students and faculty on sabbatical leave traveled to Kenya to study or teach at Daystar University near Nairobi.

With an upsurge in new students and the addition of new programs, the number of faculty rose as well. By 2000, over three-quarters of Malone's 106 faculty members had been hired during the previous decade. While the college ethos remained deeply rooted in its holiness-evangelical heritage, the institution's community of faculty-scholars became more broadly Christian during the Self years. Faculty increasingly hailed from Catholic, Lutheran, Orthodox, and Reformed, as well as evangelical, faith traditions. The diversity of

Student Life at Malone

Christian backgrounds deepened a spirit of ecumenism and *esprit de corps* among the faculty.

The General Education curriculum was modified to reflect the centrality of stewardship in a faith-filled life, although the basic template was similar to the Education for 2000 A. D. model. Students were required to enroll in General Education courses that were divided into five broad categories: Stewardship under God, Stewardship and Skills, Stewardship and the Sciences, Stewardship and Society, and a fifth component which required students to participate in a multicultural experience off campus. Given an increasingly diverse American society, college officials wanted students to develop, as noted in the school's newly revised mission statement, "an international perspective through cross-cultural experiences." The General Education package complemented major fields of study and, coupled with chapel and Student Development programs, presented multiple opportunities for a purposeful and rewarding college experience.

While undergraduate students matriculated at Malone primarily to earn a baccalaureate degree, their richest and longest-lasting memories were often made outside of the classroom. As soon as they arrived on the Malone College campus, freshmen were warmly greeted by faculty, staff, and veteran students and participated in a variety of orientation activities. Freshmen Week, as Orientation Week was originally called, included such festivities as New Student banquets, Big Brother-Big Sister events, student mixers, picnics, and hayrides. From the late 1950s until the early 1980s, freshmen were required to wear red and white beanies and participate in a variety of community-building, and sometimes humbling, activities. For one, freshmen were required to "dink" upperclassmen. That is, they swept their beanies across the tops of their elders' shoes as if to dust them. First-year students were also subjected to a variety of playful pranks. The Class of 1964, for example, dutifully scrubbed the front steps to Founders Hall in 1960. Freshman Week culminated with Kangaroo Court. Typically held off campus, Kangaroo Court was officiated by an upperclassman who meted out various "punishments" and indignities upon the hapless freshmen. By evening's end, however, first-year students were fully initiated as Pioneers.

When the provost ended freshmen "hazing" by doing away with beanies and Kangaroo Court in

the early 1980s, new activities replaced the old. By the first decade of the new millennium, the Main Event, for example, had become another beloved Pioneer tradition. The Main Event was held in late August on the Saturday before classes commenced. Returning students renewed friendships and greeted their first-year classmates on the Quad, feasted on picnic fare, and vied for prizes in a giant game of musical chairs.

The Student Activities Council (SAC), class officers, and residence life staff hosted a variety of other activities throughout the rest of the academic year. The 1960s featured Christmas and Valentine's Day banquets, Christmas decorating contests, Junior-Senior retreats, Sadie Hawkins Daze, and Pioneer Day. First held in 1966, Pioneer Day featured bed races along Harvard Avenue, a giant tug-of-war at Stadium Park, bicycle races, a skateboard obstacle course, and piano smashing. Yes, students used sledge hammers and other implements

to demolish pianos. TWIRP ("The Woman Is Required to Pay") replaced Sadie Hawkins Daze, but the premise was the same: women asked men to accompany them on a date. In 1974, Dean of Women Brenda Brenneman introduced female residents to "Ring Downs," a celebratory event that she borrowed from her alma mater, Taylor University. Reinforced by the "ring-by-Spring" mindset common at most Christian campuses across the nation, Ring Downs were a way in which newly-engaged women could share their happy news. Until College Hill and Haviland Halls were constructed, the future bride and her female classmates always gathered in Cynthia Meyers Lounge. A lit candle traveled around the circle of women. On the second rotation, the future bride blew out the candle and joyful congratulations and a variety of shenanigans ensued. Many of these earlier traditions, including Ring Downs, were abandoned or gave way to new ones.

Although Homecoming had been an annual fall staple of campus life since 1951, it was not until the winter of 1963 that a Campus Queen was selected by the student body. Judy Voltz '63 was the first to hold that honor. Court attendants were nominated and elected by members of their class, and the queen was elected by the student body

at large. Female attendants were escorted by class presidents or student council officers, all male. Shortly thereafter, Homecoming became a fall event, and every class constructed a Homecoming float and competed for "best float" honors. An annual Homecoming parade was held in downtown Canton for several years. After a short period in the 1970s during which Homecoming was once

Malone Memories

The Lord knew that Malone College was exactly where I was supposed to be. "I will instruct you and teach you in the way that you should go, I will guide you with my eyes" (Psalms 32:7). That's how I arrived in Canton from my home in southern Michigan.

From the moment I walked on Malone's campus, I met the most amazing people. Many of whom are still my dearest friends. Friends were one gift, but not the only. The professors became lifelong friends also. They took a genuine interest in my life and my walk with the Lord. To be in a class that opened in prayer was something I never took for granted.

The books I read while in college that were either assigned by a professor or referred to by a resident assistant have helped shape my walk with the Lord almost more than anything else. The scripture I memorized while at Malone laid the foundation that would carry me through the rest of my life. It is what I have built everything upon since then. I cannot express what those years meant to me. There aren't many days or weeks that go by that I am not reminded of a scripture or book or friend that I experienced at Malone.

What a gift from God when He sent me there. I have never, ever taken it for granted and count it one of the biggest blessings in my life. I would not be who I am today if it weren't for my stay at Malone.

Oh, I met my husband there too! I also became a teacher (my dream since I was in the second grade) and recently retired from teaching second grade.

Pamela Mason King, Class of 1977
Elementary Education

again held in February, Homecoming returned as an annual autumn event, although floats and parades remained a thing of the past. The college did modernize the festivities in 1985 when a Homecoming King and male representatives were finally elected to the court. Of course, Homecoming, as the name connotes, was also designated as a time to welcome returning alumni. Class reunions, gatherings with professors, a special chapel service, children's activities, and the annual alumni awards banquet brought back former students and their families to campus.

Student forms of amusement were typically chaste but amusing, as was common at most Christian colleges like Malone. In the 1970s, Fantastic Friday, or other similarly-named field days, supplanted Pioneer Day. Classes were canceled and students participated in Volkswagen-pushing contests, relay races, and tug-of-war battles. In the 1980s and beyond, "Celebrate" and a variety of spring festivals included bed races of old, tandem bicycle races, and water balloon tossing. Halloween parties, banquets, Christmas decorating contests, talent shows, concerts, intramurals, Donkey Basketball, and sporting events occupied Malone students when they were not in class or studying. On snowy days, students often took their mattresses or cafeteria trays to the hill behind Penn Hall and slid down the steep slope toward the expressway. The 1980s also saw the addition of the annual Senior banquet, Senior Recognition, an Autumn Festival, Little Sibs Weekends, Dorm Feud (a residence hall version of a popular game show), a Spring Formal…and a toga party. Yes, a toga party.

Kawfee Haus Concerts, DeVol Hall Lobby talent shows, and Little Saints Night, an alternative Halloween activity for community children, kept Malone students busy. SAC continued to sponsor hayrides, roller skating, progressive dinners, trips to Cedar Point and professional sporting events, whitewater rafting, and other off-campus excursions. Although students might complain of nothing to do on campus or headed home for the weekend, boredom was certainly not due to a lack of activities at Malone College.

Indeed, innovative Malone traditions emerged during the Self and Johnson administrations. The first Hugana Gigana Banana Split contest was organized in 1990. Teams of students dressed up in thematic costumes, choreographed a team dance or skit, and competed in a gargantuan banana-split-speed-eating contest. The event raised money for local philanthropic organizations, including the food bank. During Spirit Week in 1993, the Office of Student Development inaugurated the first "Nike Air Band" event. Nike Air Band, an archetypal Christian-college activity, is a lip-synching contest whereby teams are judged on their creative

story-telling, costumes, and song selection, as well as their collective lip-synching talents. The first rendition of an Air Band Contest at Malone was held in 1984, about the time a national lip-synching show captured the national attention. After the annual contest was renamed in 1993, winners received a can of Spam. Eventually, students competed for the coveted Golden Sneakers trophy and cash prizes. Chris Abrams, Class of 1994 and later Vice President of Student Development at Malone, was an early Nike Air Band participant. The event still fosters quintessentially "good, clean fun" at Malone to the present day.

Inspired by the bed races of old, the Student Development Office launched the Davenport Derby in 1999. Like Nike Air Band and Hugana Gigana Banana Split contests, the Davenport Derby offered students a chance to show off their creative flair. Each team decorated a couch according to a specific theme, developed a choreography, and dressed accordingly. Prizes were awarded for best theme and first and second places in the davenport races. The winning sofa received the "coveted" Golden Couch and a cash prize. Although the annual Hugana Gigana contest went moribund a few years ago, Nike Air Band and Davenport Derby are still cherished Malone traditions.

Student life also included self-governance. Student Council, originally founded in 1946, continued to represent the interests of Malone students in Canton. In 1967, the name of the association was changed to Student Senate. For a

brief period in the 1980s, the student representative organization was christened Associated Students of Malone College (ASMC), but the organization's designation soon reverted back to Student Senate. In the 1970s, Senate's cabinet gradually evolved from one that comprised a president, two vice presidents, a secretary, and a treasurer to one that included a president, vice president, and several directors. Eventually, class officers joined elected representatives as members of Student Senate. In addition to overseeing the Student Activities Council, intramurals, and the spiritual life committee, senators responded to the concerns and interests of students at Malone. They negotiated changes in visiting hours, advocated for student input in rules concerning student dress and conduct, and successfully lobbied for a recycling program on campus. Working closely with faculty and administrators, Student Senate provided vital student input in all areas of campus life.

In addition to Student Senate and student clubs, Malone students found a variety of ways to use their talents. Malone's student newspaper, *The Aviso,* began serving as the "voice" of Malone students in 1958. *The Aviso* was typically published weekly or biweekly and included features, editorials, sports updates, and a comic strip. In the early 2010s, *The Aviso* published exclusively online before printed versions began to reappear by the midpoint of the decade. The first Malone College yearbook was known as *The Malonian* for the 1956 and 1957 editions. In 1958 and thereafter, the publication was entitled the *Philos*. The *Philos* captured student life at Malone until 2008, the last two years being digitized versions, before it went defunct. In addition to *The Aviso* and *Philos*, Malone students also published a student directory known as the *Phiz*. The *Phiz* still exists, although it has been fully online since 2006.

The college provided opportunities that complemented students' academic gifts. The *Livret* published students' poems, short stories, and other creative writing pieces. In 1994, the name of the literary journal was changed to *From the Catacombs*, but the purpose, which was to foster students' writing talents, remained the same. The presence of debate and speech squads waxed and waned during the college era, but the Forensics team, founded in 1992, was active for nearly a quarter of a century. Members won awards at the local and national levels.

Those who excelled academically were recognized in a number of ways. In the early 1960s, Malone's top students were recognized as Honor Guides. Selected by the Dean of Students and attired in special blazers, Honor guides served as hosts to prospective students and other campus guests. In 1964, Malone's first class of "Who's Who in American Colleges and Universities" was chosen. The eight honorees that year were Judith Haver, Robert Huffman, Judith Ley, Rebecca Lafferty, Marion Mazzarella, Arthur Moyer, David R. Van Valkenburg, and Alma Wolford. In 1979, the annual Senior Recognition Banquet was inaugurated. The top senior in every academic major was recognized at a special year-end banquet held at the end of Spring Semester.

Of course, as a Christian institution, Malone College expected its students, faculty, staff, and administrators to abide by requisite standards of moral and ethical behavior in and beyond the classroom. But the institution also expected members of the Malone community to value and respect each other. In the preamble to the school's "Community Responsibilities" statement, the college catalog noted in 1992:

> Malone is more than just an organization; it is a community of persons which includes administrators, faculty, supportive staff, and all students enrolled in any of the classes offered by the college on its campus. We recognize that our students represent a wide range of backgrounds, attitudes, needs and goals. Therefore, as a liberal arts college that is distinctively Christian, Malone views each person as an individual with certain responsibilities to the college community.

In time, every Malone student, regardless of his or her faith commitment, was required to sign the school's Community Responsibilities agreement. Although the community agreement seemed to mirror old forms of legalism, it was rooted in a concern for the spiritual, emotional, and physical well-being of its students. Not only were drinking and smoking on campus forbidden, but other social behaviors were curtailed too. Sometimes these social constraints reflected prevailing attitudes found in evangelical circles. Often, the restrictions loosened over time. Card playing, for instance, was not permitted until 1970, and women could not wear slacks in the classroom until 1972. There were no co-ed floors in residence halls, although men and women sometimes did reside in the same building. Fox Hall regularly housed men on the east side of the second floor, but a locked door separated them from women living on the west side. Visiting hours

were restricted and occurred a few times per year until rules were relaxed over time. Until 1977, female residents were confined to their residence hall after certain hours. First-year women were expected to be in their dormitories by 11:00 p.m. on weeknights and midnight on weekends. Curfew for older female students was midnight on weeknights and 2:00 a.m. on weekends. There was no curfew for male students, except for first-semester freshmen. Title IX led to the elimination of gender-based restrictions at Malone, but shifting attitudes within the larger Christian community contributed to a relaxation of restrictions as well.

One of the more controversial changes in policy involved dancing. Dances were forbidden for most of the Malone College era, although "unofficial" dances off campus were organized from time to time. In 1987, over one hundred Malone students attended a non-sanctioned dance. Chagrined at their peers' behavior, a few non-attendees complained that the dance had violated community standards. However, Malone eventually modified this policy as well. In 2000, the Board of Trustees approved a new dance policy, and the first official dance at Malone College was held on October 12, 2000. Although some constituents were displeased with the change, the new policy was instituted with relatively little fuss or fanfare.

Of course, this does not mean that Malone College was lax in enforcing community standards. In 1995, *The Aviso* reported that students were fined $15.00 for swearing, $20.00 for visitation violations, and $50.00 for first-time alcohol policy offenses. Those caught with intoxicating drink were also required to attend counseling sessions and perform community service. Subsequent violations could lead to suspension or dismissal. While many of the regulations at Malone were sacrosanct, administrators and faculty tried to offer a measure of grace. Christian love, reconciliation, and hospitality characterized student life at Malone College, even if imperfectly at times.

VII: Remaining Steadfast

In 1994, Dr. Self accepted an appointment to serve as president of Seattle Pacific University. Ronald Johnson, who had served as acting president after Gordon Werkema stepped down in 1988, filled in as interim again. Fortunately, he was soon appointed to serve as Malone's eleventh president in 1994. Dr. Johnson was the third and final president during the Malone College period to hail from a Friends background. President Johnson served for thirteen years, longer than any other president during the liberal arts college era.

Ronald Johnson's appointment as president in 1994 was particularly fitting. Like Presidents Wollam, Osborne, and Spring before him, Dr. Johnson first arrived at the school as a first-year student. Highly respected among Friends and faculty, Johnson brought his unwavering Christian faith, a steadfast loyalty to the institution, and a sure hand to his role as chief executive officer of the institution. Over the course of his

thirteen-year administration, President Johnson, affectionately dubbed "Ron Jon" by Malone students, oversaw significant growth in student enrollment, academic programming, endowments, and campus construction and acquisitions.

Malone's student population continued to expand during the Johnson years. Between 1994 and 2007, the school saw a nearly twenty percent increase in enrollment. During that period, the student population rose from 1,876 to 2,385. With a growth rate of 173%, graduate school enrollment accounted for over half of the overall increase. Malone College was still mirroring a national trend among Christian institutions of higher learning throughout the 1990s and 2000s. As public and private colleges and universities became more secularized, with a few seemingly hostile to religious belief, their Christian counterparts offered a welcome alternative. Christian colleges and universities like Malone were among the fastest growing institutions of higher learning in the nation. Since Malone was accredited by the same governing body as secular colleges and universities, prospective students and their parents were assured of an academically rigorous, as well as a Christ-centered, education.

Although the addition of College Hill and Heritage Halls in the mid-1990s had eased the student housing crunch, existing accommodations could not keep up with demand. During the 1995–96 academic year, women were housed in Penn-Gurney-Barclay (PGB) Hall, and lounges

in Woolman-Whittier-Fox (WWF) Hall were converted into rooms for female residents. That same year, campus housing for married students, which had been available since the construction of College Hill, was dropped to make room for more single residents, and, even then, not enough rooms were available. Market Ridge apartments, located just down the street from the college, were secured from time to time for the overflow. To accommodate the growing demand for on-campus housing, Laura Smith Haviland Hall was constructed in 1999, completing the enclosure of what became known as the "Quad"—the grassy area between Haviland, Heritage, and WWF Halls.

The opening of Haviland Hall was a significant marker in Malone College's history. It was the first time since the move to Canton that a residence hall, or any campus building for that matter, had been named in honor of a woman. Although Friends had long "testified" about the equality of men and women, and Esther Baird Hall had graced the Cleveland Bible College grounds, no building on the Canton campus paid tribute to any spiritually "weighty" women until Haviland Hall opened its doors. The oversight was

glaring. So much so that six years later, College Hill was renamed DeVol Hall in honor of Isabella French DeVol. Dr. DeVol, another Friend, was a medical missionary to China and mother-in-law of President Everett Cattell.

Naming the building after Laura Haviland, a nineteenth-century abolitionist from Michigan, was additionally noteworthy for other reasons. For one, she was the first Quaker with roots in the Evangelical Friends Church: Eastern Region to be so honored. Haviland Hall was also notable because it was the first intentionally co-educational residence hall on campus. Although men and women were housed in PGB and WWF periodically over the years, these were always stopgap measures during housing shortages, and male and female students were confined behind locked doors to assigned areas. In Haviland Hall, floors were designated either male or female, but the community remained inclusive. The experiment was short-lived, however, and by the Fall of 2000, only women were living in Haviland Hall. Although students at the time bemoaned the loss of a unique

community, there has yet to be another co-ed residence hall on campus.

As Malone's enrollment continued to expand during the first decade of the new millennium, the demand for residential housing once again became acute, and plans to construct a new residence hall on campus commenced near the end of the Johnson administration in 2007. Dudley S. Blossom III Hall opened its doors in January 2009 to accommodate male residents. Interestingly, Blossom Hall is the only residential building on campus, other than Heritage Hall, not named in honor of a Quaker. However, the Blossom family donated generously toward its construction, hence its current moniker.

As the number of undergraduate, degree-completion, and graduate students enrolled at Malone increased, so too did the array of program offerings. In 2005, for example, one of the fastest growing majors, zoo and wildlife biology, was added to the menu of majors at Malone. Graduate degrees in business administration, counseling, and nursing were inaugurated during the Johnson years. The Malone College Management Program (MCMP), which continued to attract hundreds of students annually, welcomed its one hundredth class during the 1996–97 academic year. Some within the Malone community were concerned about an increasing emphasis on the professions, but administrators and faculty remained committed to the humanities and a solid grounding in the liberal arts via the General Education component. Following in the footsteps of their predecessors, Malone professors teaching in the arts, sciences,

and professions promoted a liberal arts-based, Christ-centered approach to higher education.

Faculty took the lead in advocating for the liberal arts. During a faculty business meeting in 2000, Dr. Douglas Henry, professor of philosophy, stirred his colleagues to collective action when he invited the Malone College community to think more intentionally about its historic mission and the school's Christian and Quaker legacy. He challenged faculty to consider what was unique about the institution and how that might be reflected more explicitly in its ongoing mission. Malone's faculty took his entreaty to heart.

In 2002, the General Education Committee began crafting new Educational Goals to articulate an academically rigorous, intellectually stimulating, and Biblically-based General Education menu. The intent, as always, was to ground students in the liberal arts in order to nurture their spiritual growth, foster character development, and enhance their critical thinking and analytical skills. As members of the General Education Committee deliberated, it became clear that their efforts to develop a comprehensive liberal arts curriculum might be hampered without a guiding moral compass. Thus, in the Summer of 2002, the General Education Committee put its work on hold and appointed an *ad hoc* committee to flesh out Malone's historical core values. These became known as Foundational Principles. A year later, the Foundational Principles committee was asked to revise the mission statement to better complement the embryonic Foundational Principles and Educational Goals. Reflecting the consensus-building heritage of the Friends, the Malone community-at-large vetted the revised mission statement and Foundational Principles documents collectively. After a number of focus groups, which included faculty, staff, and administrators, were conducted and the documents revised, the new mission statement and Foundational Principles were approved by the Board of Trustees in 2004.

Malone College
Students at
Work

With the revision of the mission statement and completion of the Foundational Principles, the General Education Committee now had a clearer road map to formulate a set of Educational Goals and revamp the General Education package. Once completed, a community conversation about the goals and General Education menu led to additional tweaking and refining. With their work completed, the General Education Committee submitted the Educational Goals to the Board of Trustees for approval in 2006. The goals ensured that assessment and learning outcomes were easier to track and adjust, and the new General Education menu better complemented the school's major fields of study. More importantly, Malone's Educational Goals operationalized and enhanced the newly-articulated mission of Malone, which stated that the missional purpose of the school was "to provide students with an education based on biblical faith in order to develop men and women in intellectual maturity, wisdom, and Christian faith who are committed to serving the church, community, and world."

The centerpiece of the new General Education package was a discussion-based capstone course, "Faith in the World Seminar." As previously noted, a culminating theology class for seniors had long been an essential component in Malone's General Education menu. Over the years, Malone students had been required to enroll in such theology capstone courses as "God, the World, and Man," "Faith and Contemporary Problems," and "Faith and Personal Ethics." However, the new capstone requirement gave students the option to enroll in one of several topical seminars that were more interdisciplinary in nature. The purpose of the seminar was to explore "what it means to think and live faithfully in our world by undertaking an in-depth study of an important issue." Upper-level students enrolled in a wide range of Faith in the World seminars. A sampling of topics included Living Well in a Car Culture, Understanding and Responding to Loss, Film and the American Dream, Work and Vocation, and the Seven Deadly Sins, among others. Seniors not only were challenged with "some of the best Christian thinking" on a particular issue, but they were also given the opportunity to "reflect on God's call on his/her life."

81

The process of hewing missional values and educational goals *communally* was perhaps the most significant outcome of the six-year journey that culminated in the completion of the mission statement, Foundational Principles, Educational Goals, and General Education menu. From the beginning, President Johnson supported and the Malone community embraced collaborative, grassroots, campus-wide efforts to draw from the school's Christian and institutional heritage in revising and even reimagining Malone College's liberal arts requirements. Yet, this is perhaps not surprising. Countless volumes of faculty minutes in the Malone archives reveal that shared governance is another long-standing tradition at Emma and Walter's school. Although parliamentary procedures of the modern era have understandably seeped into the collective decision-making processes at Malone to accommodate an expanding employee population, the traditional Quaker values of consensus-building and unity continued to inform governance and curricular issues at Malone College.

This is not to suggest that consensus was always achieved, but generally, President Johnson and his cabinet typically solicited the voices of faculty

and staff. This was also true in 2000 when the Johnson Administration laid out plans for academic restructuring. The central administrative model whereby department heads reported directly to the provost was becoming increasingly unwieldy as the institution's enrollments and program offerings grew in size and complexity. By the late 1990s, the Johnson Administration had begun to experiment with new reporting channels when an academic dean was appointed. However, adding merely one administrative position seemed to be insufficient to meet the organizational needs of the campus, and the post was abandoned in 2000. The new decentralized structure comprised of "schools," each headed by a dean, was instituted in 2001. The six new schools were grouped according to academic disciplines and included Arts and Sciences, Business, Continuing Studies, Education, Nursing, and Theology. The largest of the schools, Arts and Sciences, was divided into two divisions: Humanities and Natural and Behavioral Sciences. The intent was to offer another layer of administrative oversight and ease somewhat the increasingly burdensome responsibilities of the chief academic officer.

Given the new administrative structure, the president's cabinet suggested that the college might be rechristened as a university as part of the reorganization plan. Although several faculty raised a few concerns about placing academic departments under the umbrella of six schools, there was wider unease about designating the college as a university. Malone faculty, especially those representing the School of Arts and Sciences but also those hailing from other departments, were troubled that the new title would dilute the Christian liberal arts focus of the institution and diminish its academic standing. In keeping with a tradition of shared governance at Malone College, President Johnson was attentive to the concerns of the faculty, found their claims to be reasonable, and deferred the renaming of the college for the remainder of his tenure.

A high regard for faculty contributions to the intellectual and spiritual life of the institution during the Johnson administration was evident elsewhere. In 1998, the Distinguished Faculty Awards for Excellence in Teaching, Scholarship/Creative Expression, and Service were inaugurated. The first recipients were Professors Eugene Collins for teaching, Duane Watson for scholarship, and Arnold Fritz for service. Similar awards were presented annually to supporting and administrative staff.

The college also instituted several faculty programs to foster professional growth and development. While faculty development had been led in earlier years by Professors Burley Smith and Kim Phipps (now president of Messiah College), a new series of programs was established as the new millennium dawned. In 1999, Academic Dean Beth Doriani and Dr. Stephen Moroney introduced and taught a semester-long Faith-Integration seminar for first-year faculty. Shortly thereafter, the first-year faculty program was revamped and expanded. Building on an existing peer-mentor program, the college launched a monthly first-year faculty seminar in 2001. The new program did not replace the Faith-Integration seminar. Instead, the seminar was offered to second-year faculty. Under the leadership of Professors David Entwistle, Suzanne Nicholson, Stephen Moroney, and Christina Schnyders, the first-year and second-year faculty professional development programs continue to serve new professors at Malone to the present day. In 2007, the college devoted new resources to faculty development when the Board of Trustees approved a part-time Faculty Development Director position. First held by Dr. Matthew Phelps for nine years, Dr. T. C. Ham was appointed to the position in 2016. In partnership with the Faculty Development Committee, the Faculty Development Director oversees a variety of activities, seminars, and retreats that cultivate intellectual inquiry, scholarship, best practices in teaching, spiritual development, and camaraderie.

Professional development programs, sabbaticals, and summer grants enabled Malone faculty to engage in scholarly research, craft creative works,

publish books and journal articles, present at academic conferences, and participate in a wide range of professional organizations and activities. Testifying to the quality of Malone professors, four faculty were awarded Fulbright Scholarships between 2004 and 2011. In 2004, Dr. Scott Waalkes traveled to Bahrain where he served as a Visiting Fulbright Scholar in the Department of Economics and Finance at the University of Bahrain. Dr. James Brownlee taught at Russian American University in the Department of Literature and Philology in 2005. Dr. Ken Stoltzfus received a Fulbright Lecturing/Research Award in 2010 and also traveled to Russia where he examined faith-based responses to substance abuse in Russia. Dr. Jack Ballard spent the first half of 2013 as a Fulbright Scholar at Daystar University in Kenya, where he explored "The Music Industry and African Musical Culture." Several other Malone faculty were Fulbright semi-finalists.

Not only did faculty scholarship and professional development blossom during Johnson's tenure, but the Honors Program, after a six-year gestation period, was inaugurated in 2000. Already in 1994, Provost Robert Suggs and a student-led committee were discussing the implementation of an honors program for high-ability students at Malone. The topic was revisited in 1998, but discussions came to naught. It was another two years before the program was finally established. Launched in 2000, the Honors Program took shape during Dr. Diane Chambers' tenure as director from 2001 to 2016. The purpose of Malone's Honors Program "is to support the College's intellectually gifted and highly motivated students, to create a community of students and faculty engaged in serious, substantive, and sustained critical inquiry, and to underscore the College's commitment to academic excellence." Honors students enrolled in designated honors sections of general education courses, a sophomore seminar, and a junior seminar. The culminating requirement was a two-semester thesis project that was defended before a student-selected thesis committee, presented to the Malone community, and published or digitized for inclusion in the Cattell Library.

Even as new programs and faculty lines were added, the college's motto, "Christ's Kingdom First," and its doctrinal foundation were unaltered. Students were still expected to abide by the institution's "Attitudinal and Behavioral Expectations" and sign the community agreement. Although Founders Week was not observed as it had been in the past, an annual Missions Week or Spiritual Life Week was embedded in the institutional calendar.

The presence of Pastor Randy Heckert and Linda Leon enriched the spiritual climate on campus. Not only did they oversee biweekly chapels, offer spiritual guidance, and mentor Malone students, but they provided comfort and solace during times of difficulty. When the campus tragically lost beloved members of the community during the Johnson Administration, including Associate Dean of Students Steve Everett, First Lady Marjorie Johnson, and far too many students, the Campus Ministries team and the entire Malone family consoled each other with their prayers and faithful presence. On September 11, 2001, when classes were canceled due to the unfolding crisis in New York City, central Pennsylvania, and the nation's capital, the Campus Ministries team could be found praying with and reassuring Malone students.

The value of living and praying together in Christian community was not lost on Malone students. In 2004, a few of them, with permission from the Student Development Office, sought to live together in what became known as a Discipleship House. The first Discipleship House was originally an off-campus housing option for male students who wanted to grow in their relationship with Christ and be held accountable by others. Eventually, a Discipleship House opened for women. Students living in each Discipleship House went through a selection process conducted by their peers and Malone faculty, corralled their resources, budgeted their expenses, took turns purchasing their groceries, cooked together, broke bread in community, and lived in fellowship intentionally and devotionally. Although the Discipleship Houses disbanded after ten years, they were exemplars of faithful living in Christian community. And, perhaps, this experiment in communal living will reemerge in the not-too-distant future.

Not all students felt as connected to the larger Malone community as others. Commuting students felt less embedded in campus life or found the travel to evening or weekend events burdensome. In 1996, commuters were asked by members of the *Philos* staff to share the drawbacks and benefits of living at home. One commuter bemoaned her "long drives after play practice at 1:30 in the morning." Another found it "hard to meet people." Of course, they both cited the advantages,

such as "home-cooked meals" and no visitation hours. To ensure that commuters "found their place" at Malone, Senate established a director for commuting students in the late 1970s. During the Johnson years, a specially-designated group, M.C.T.A. (Malone College Traveler's Association) was founded for students who lived off campus. Not surprisingly, Froggy's Café and Regula Café became gathering spots for commuters. Eventually, a commuter lounge was set aside as a campus "home" for nonresidential students. Commuter Bible studies offered another outlet for non-residential students who were seeking fellowship with other "traveling" Christians.

Although minority and international students had been enrolling at Malone University since its founding in the late nineteenth century, students of color and international status were often isolated or lonely. A variety of clubs for international and African-American students had been established

over the course of the school's history, but these tended to be ephemeral in nature and depended on too few minority faculty and staff to ensure their longevity and stability. In 1996,

Brenda Stevens was appointed as Malone College's first Director of Multicultural Services in response to the dearth of amenities and programs for minority students. The purpose of Multicultural Services Office was to "build and maintain a community that is more inclusive of underrepresented American ethnic minorities and international students." Thus, Mrs. Stevens not only planned activities and events specifically for the men and women her office served, but also campus-wide opportunities for all Malone students to encourage a greater appreciation for cultural diversity and foster meaningful conversation and understanding throughout Malone College.

For both good and ill, the ubiquitous presence of technology on campus generated new spaces for conversations during the Johnson era. Gone were the days of computer key punch cards, electronic typewriters, and landline telephones. Faculty were supplied with personal computers, Malone employees and students were assigned designated email accounts, advanced screening and testing instruments were added to science and nursing labs, and, with the increasing popularity of laptop computers, wireless Internet accessibility made studying anywhere on campus easier. When the bookstore moved from Cattell Library to its new digs in the Brehme Centennial Center in 1994, the library space was repurposed as a computer lab.

Of course, technology offered its own set of troublesome distractions as well as benefits. The October 26, 2000, issue of *The Aviso* reported that cell phone use was "plaguing" campus. When given the choice of reading *Plato's Republic* or texting, students often chose the latter. Video games, My Space, and blogs provided new social spaces and popular diversions for Malone students. Of course, Facebook, which arrived on campus shortly after it was launched at Harvard University in 2004, was a game changer. *The Aviso* observed Facebook's growing popularity in its pages in 2005 and, with addition of Twitter in 2006, mobile devices became increasingly omnipresent in the residence hall, classroom, and even chapel. Whenever Provost Wilbert Friesen spoke in chapel, he asked the students to pull out their cell phones, raise them in the air, and turn them off. Even with bursts of laughter rippling throughout the sanctuary, most students complied.

Not only did the technological footprint on campus expand under the leadership of Clark Hoopes and John Koshmider, among others, but the physical space was enlarged as well. By the end of the 1990s, a classroom crunch accompanied the

residential housing shortage. A temporary structure, known as Timken Annex, provided classroom and faculty office space until Mitchell Hall opened in 1999. Named in honor of Malone alumni Edward and Ruth Alma Mosher Mitchell, the new building housed Silk Auditorium, classrooms, and the Departments of Education and Business. Construction and new acquisitions continued unabated for the remainder of Johnson's tenure. In 2004, the Wellness Center, which adjoined the east side of Osborne Hall, opened, and construction on Ralph Regula Hall, named in honor of a local congressman, was completed three years later. Regula Hall resolved the shortage of laboratory, classroom, and office space for the nursing program.

The Malone campus also expanded via acquisition. When the First Christian Church congregation put up its facility for sale, Malone College administrators made an offer. For years, the college had rented the church's sanctuary for chapel services and the second floor for the Weaver Child Development Center. Purchased in 2006, the building was renamed the Ronald G. Johnson Center for Worship and The Fine Arts in honor of the school's eleventh president.

This was an especially fitting honor since Dr. Johnson announced his decision to retire just as the college was preparing to take possession of the Johnson Center. President Johnson's departure in 2007 marked the end of an era in more than one way. By the time he retired, almost all of his faculty peers who had been hired in the 1960s and 1970s had stepped down. Jack Hazen, who marked his fortieth anniversary at Malone in 2007, was the notable exception. Many of the departing faculty had served Malone for a quarter of a century or more and remained steadfastly dedicated to the institution and its students. Professor Eugene Collins, a Cleveland Bible College alumnus who had been appointed professor of Biblical studies in 1967, poignantly captured the sentiments of his colleagues upon his own retirement in 1999: "I love you all. No one anywhere can ever replace you."

Johnson's departure also coincided with the fiftieth anniversary of the college's relocation to Canton. The slogan which commemorated the milestone, "Three Centuries, Two Cities, One Calling," aptly captured the journey and mission of Malone College. Certainly, the half century in Canton was marked by significant growth and transformation. Enrollment, program, and infrastructure expansion were the most visible signs of change. However, a renewed commitment to Walter and Emma Malone's calling and to their founding principles also characterized the Malone College years.

The institution was not immune to problems during the college era. Women were conspicuously underrepresented on the faculty, in administrative posts, and on the Board of Trustees throughout most of the period. Minority and international students sometimes felt marginalized. The energy crisis of the 1970s and beyond contributed to recurring financial woes. Student conduct and regulations were contested well into the new millennium. At times, national and regional events disrupted life on campus. Malone College canceled classes after the tragic shootings at nearby Kent State University in 1970, the slaying of Vice President Richard Chambers during a botched car-jacking in 1978, and in the aftermath of the September 11, 2001, tragedy. And, yet, during these and other times of crises, students, staff, faculty, and administrators bonded, ministered to each other, and came together in love and prayer.

Honors student Autumn Berry Terry, Class of 2015, who wrote her thesis on cultural changes at Malone College during the Everett Cattell years observed, "Malone definitely [experienced] peaks

and troughs, but one thing that has seemed to remain constant is Malone's care for its people. There are always complaints about food, facilities, etc. no matter the generation, but 'the people here' is always a huge reason behind why people choose to come to Malone and why they continue to love it."

"The people here" who shaped Malone College are legion. Like Professor Arnold Fritz, who helped found the Stark Wilderness Center, co-organized the annual "Gold Rush" non-profit fund-raiser, and led biology students on trips to Costa Rica. Or Sandra Johnson, who was the chief organizer behind Freshman Orientation Week, Worldview Forum, Parents Weekend, and a host of other events during her four-decade tenure at Malone. Or Tim Laino, Class of 2009, who made Christmas cards for every student on campus during his freshman year. Tim was widely known as the "Birthday Guy" because he also crafted birthday cards for each Malone student. Or Kathy Geosits, who came to Malone in 2001 as the dining hall cashier. Much to the astonishment of incoming

freshmen and transfers, Miss Kathy, as she is known, quickly learned and remembered the name of every Malone student who dined on campus. She still does.

Extraordinary people all.

Of course, few have been as fondly remembered as Malone's favorite "pal," John Edward "Hutch" Hutchens. Born with Down syndrome on May 27, 1925, Hutch became a fixture on campus between 1959 and 1981. Hutch, who walked daily to Malone from his nearby home, volunteered in the library, dined with students in the cafeteria, participated in campus events, attended commencement ceremonies, and provided halftime entertainment at basketball games, whether shooting hoops, conducting the pep band, or leading students in his favorite cheer: "W-A-L-S-H: Malone!" Never was there a more loyal fan of the Pioneers than John Hutchens. A perpetual "freshman," his picture appeared annually with first-year students in the college yearbook, right where he belonged. Among his friends.

In honor of his 56th birthday and two-decade presence at Malone College, Canton Mayor Stanley Cmich proclaimed May 20, 1981, as John "Hutch" Hutchens Day. The 1981 *Philos* made note of Hutch's inestimable value at Malone: "John Hutchens has been a part of the College for over 20 years and to most, it is hard to think of Malone without 'Hutch.' He has worked in the college library straightening chairs and books and has become the subject of ample term papers, the favorite half-time entertainer at games, and the one personality on campus most likely never to be forgotten." Hutch died on August 17, 1985, at age 60. The John E. Hutchens Scholarship was established

at Malone in his memory, and he was posthumously inducted into the Malone College Athletics Hall of Fame in 1989.

That abiding sense of hospitality, generosity, and genuine concern for others characterized the Malone College era, as it would the university era as well.

Ronald Johnson's resignation signaled the close of the Malone College era. A few months after Dr. Johnson retired, his successor, President Gary Streit, appointed a "Blue Ribbon Commission on University Status," comprised of Malone faculty, administrators, staff, and trustees, to consider changing the institution's designation from college to university. While the college had functioned under a university structure since 2001, its name had not reflected the change. Although some within the Malone community were resistant, especially those still concerned about the possible diminution of the school's historical liberal arts emphasis, the Board of Trustees approved the name change the following year.

In 2008, Emma and Walter Malone's school was rechristened "Malone University."

Chapter 5: The Christian University (2008–present)

Malone University

Every year, Malone University was abuzz with activity during Homecoming. Alumni, parents, siblings, and friends of the university joined Malone students and employees for worship, reunions, seminars, games, food, fun, and fellowship. Homecoming Weekend 2016 was no different. Fortunately, the weather cooperated. The skies were clear, the vibrant hues of fall were just beginning to brighten the foliage on campus, and the temperatures were seasonally warm and pleasant. All the makings for a memorable Homecoming.

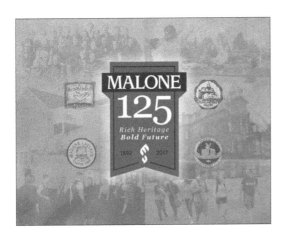

However, the 2016 edition of Homecoming weekend was particularly notable. The school was observing its 125th academic year, and Malone was immersed in quasquicentennial festivities. As always, the annual alumni awards banquet offered an opportunity for reflection, remembrance, and acclamation. Ever since former Cleveland Bible College President Worthy A. Spring '26 received the first Alumnus of the Year award in 1962, the school had annually recognized alumni of deep faith who had contributed to the school, church, and larger society. On October 7, 2016, President David A. King and Director of Alumni Relations Deborah Murray

Robinson '76 bestowed distinguished alumni honors upon five remarkable graduates of the university at the alumni banquet. Teresa Purses '86, Jane Miller '97, Jerome West '08, Dustin White '07, and Jamie White '10 were duly lauded for their extraordinary accomplishments and acts of service.

As exceptional as the alumni honorees were, President King ensured that the 2016 alumni banquet would be one of the most memorable in Malone University's history. In recognition of the institution's 125th anniversary, Dr. King thought it timely to invite former Malone presidents to participate in the celebration. Four of the five still-living past presidents, Lon D. Randall, E. Arthur Self, Ronald G. Johnson, and Gary W. Streit, made their way back to Malone University for the alumni banquet. All had served as president during the Malone College era, and each had contributed to the growth of the school. At one point, the four men encircled the current officeholder and lifted Dr. King and Malone University in prayer. Afterward, Dr. King reflected, "I am humbled by the poignancy of our moment in prayer together. Each of these men made their mark on our rich heritage, and I am honored to carry Malone into a bold future."

President King's sanguine reflection was an encouraging counterpoint to the challenges the institution faced at the opening of the university era. A crisis in the nation's financial sector, which emerged as Gary Streit was assuming his responsibilities as president in 2007, reached its nadir around the time Malone College became Malone University in the autumn of 2008. The abrupt departure of President Streit in 2010, a revolving door of key administrators, volatility in enrollment numbers, budget woes, and painful cuts in staffing and programming were unexpected setbacks. Without the staunchly committed faculty and staff, a loyal community of alumni and friends of Malone, and an abiding Christian faith that permeated the campus, Walter and Emma Malone's school might have been irrevocably destabilized. Instead, collective perseverance and prayer sustained the university, and Malone University carried on.

❦ ❧

The opening year of the Malone University era, despite a troubled economy nationally, seemed to be an especially propitious one. Blossom Hall opened its doors to residential students, a new roadway connecting the Johnson Center to the main campus was dedicated, efforts to purchase the adjacent Jewish synagogue and property were underway, and, in August 2009, the campus community welcomed the highest number of graduate and undergraduate students (2,638) ever to enroll at Malone University or its antecedents. Faculty

published books and presented scholarly research to national acclaim, the annual student research symposium was launched, and Malone graduates thrived in their respective vocations. The men's cross country program continued apace with three consecutive national championships, and a highly successful men's and women's swimming and diving program was established. The future looked bright.

By the time Wilbert Friesen was appointed as interim president in February 2010, the tide was beginning to turn. Enrollment began its slow decline during the 2010–11 academic year. The purchase of Temple Israel and nine acres of its surrounding property, rising fixed and healthcare costs, and a global recession constrained the university's financial health and taxed the administrative skills of Dr. Friesen. Friesen, who had served for less than two years as Malone's provost before he found himself as placeholder in the president's office, partnered with Provost Donald Tucker and a capable leadership team to navigate the turbulent waters ahead. Dr. Friesen's faith, determination, and resilience, coupled with the dedication of the Malone community at large, ensured that the university would prevail despite the obstacles.

In 2011, the Board of Trustees began its search for a new president in earnest. After interviewing several qualified candidates, the board appointed David A. King as the university's thirteenth president. Dr. King served in a variety of posts, including Provost, at Eastern University, a sister Christian institution, before he began his term at Malone on January 1, 2012. President King was

drawn to the university after reading Malone's Foundational Principles and its emphasis on the integration of faith, learning, and experiential activism. Like his interim predecessor before him, President King inherited many of the difficulties that emerged at the start of the decade. Yet, he viewed his new position as a "divine appointment," saw great promise in Emma and Walter Malone's school, and found an abundance of reasons to be optimistic.

For one thing, the commitment to excellence in academics and Christian service at Malone University was uncompromised throughout the King era. Graduate and degree-completion programs offered advanced studies in business, counseling, education, management, nursing, and organizational leadership. The General Education menu for undergraduates was revised in 2014, in part due to fiscal issues, but the reduction in requirements enabled students to double major or take on a minor or two, such as Athletic Training, Biblical Languages, Economics, Gender Studies, Marine Biology, Peace and Reconciliation, and others. Several new undergraduate majors were

added, including Creative Writing, Christian Worship, Criminal and Restorative Justice, Environmental Studies, Finance, Global and International Studies, Graphic Design and Digital Arts, Marketing, and, in partnership with The University of Akron, Engineering. Many of the new majors added during the university years were particularly distinctive in nature.

For instance, the Creative Writing Program at Malone, founded in 2010, prepared students with talents in the written word as future book authors, editors, poets, teachers, and writers. The program awarded Creative Writing Fellowships, and sponsored the Writers Guild, an annual Creative

Summer Academic Camps

To spark an interest in baccalaureate pursuits and life at Malone University, the school began hosting academic summer camps in 2014. Academic summer camps gave middle school and high school students a chance to explore an area of interest with Malone faculty and other professionals. Malone University scheduled a variety of academic camps in 2017.

- Applied and Scientific Psychology
- Chamber Music
- Computer Science
- Creative Writing
- Jazz Workshop
- Nursing
- Science Careers
- Theatre
- Worship Music
- Zoo & Wildlife Biology

Writing contest, and the Malone University Writers Series. The Writers Series hosted several visiting authors who conducted master writing classes, held informal conversations with students, and participated in public readings and discussions of their works. Over sixty-five visiting writers had been on campus by 2017.

The Criminal and Restorative Justice (CRJ) and Environmental Studies majors paid homage, albeit indirectly, to the Malone legacy of social activism and Christian stewardship. The CRJ major was a case in point. One of the few institutions of higher learning nationally that explicitly focused on restorative as well as criminal justice, Malone faculty designed the Criminal and Restorative Justice program to prepare students to think "beyond the simple idea of punishing criminal behavior." Instead, students examined effective ways both to support those who had been harmed and to restore "the offender within society after restitution" was made. To reinforce learning outside of the classroom, CRJ majors and other interested students were invited to attend weekly Spiritual Formation Opportunities and periodic book discussions to consider the implications of restorative justice in American society.

Like the CRJ program, the Environmental Studies major was interdisciplinary, and, in keeping with long-standing Malone values, emphasized the importance and consequential blessings of Christian stewardship and Creation care. Although the bulk of the coursework for the major was embedded in the sciences, students scrutinized the health and vitality of both urban and "natural" landscapes and considered the impact of

humankind on the local and global environment. Malone's partnership with Au Sable Institute for Environmental Studies enabled students to enroll in field courses in Michigan, Washington, Costa Rica, and India. Faculty forged Criminal and Restorative Justice, Environmental Studies, and other new majors in ways that prepared students for their vocational calling and, as noted in the Foundational Principles, fostered a learning community that manifested concern for others *and* the world they inhabited.

To cultivate deeper conversations about the Christian faith and calling beyond the classroom, Dr. Bryan Hollon, professor of theology, founded the Center for Christian Faith & Culture in 2012 to "explore the wisdom of the Christian intellectual tradition in order to foster theological literacy, prayerful contemplation, and faithful reasoning within the Church, the academy, and the other areas of professional life." The first event hosted by the center was the Bicentennial Symposium in July 2012. The symposium commemorated the two hundredth anniversary of the founding of Ohio Yearly Meeting, known after 1971 as Evangelical Friends Church: Eastern Region. Several Malone faculty, alumni, and friends of the university presented scholarly papers on the history of the denomination during the two-day conference. Since then, the center has sponsored an array of events from Woolman Lectures to pastors' luncheons, prayer workshops, Constitution Day forums, and a variety of lectures and seminars. Usually open to the public, CCFC events offered Malone students an opportunity to connect classroom learning with absorbing insights gleaned from Christian academics and theologians.

As always, Malone student-scholars flourished in the classroom, laboratory, and studio. The Honors Program cultivated the talents of high-ability students and, happily, found a permanent home in Malone's library after Regula Hall was completed in 2007. The third floor of Cattell

Malone Memories

In August of 2011 I arrived at the pearly gates of academia after an 8-hour drive from Philadelphia, and was greeted in the pouring rain by an obnoxious, seemingly unnecessarily excited mob of screaming students welcoming me to my new temporary home. That day I joined the Malone community as a fully constructed (or so I thought), confident, self-righteous 18-year old who, quite honestly, was slightly annoyed by the over-extended personalities I met those first hours on campus. But, little did I know, I needed every, single one of those people. I needed their passion, I needed them to care, and I would need that community to uphold me as I underwent holistic reconstruction.

Friends, community, and advocates, I have realized, are life's greatest gifts, and one of my best friends became so in a rather unexpected way. Soon after arriving to campus, I was paired with an upper-class student, Victoria Bankhead, through Multicultural Student Services' Smart Start program. What I at first assumed would be a routine, strictly-business relationship with my mentor, blossomed into a beautiful friendship. Victoria, along with Mrs. Brenda Stevens, not only got me quickly connected to campus, but continued to inspire me to reach my highest potential socially, spiritually, and academically, even after graduation.

I cannot fully illustrate the magnitude of the impact that my Malone experience has had on me, from relationships with my roommates, my counselor, the dining hall staff, campus safety, to the opportunities to serve in my community. However, my final year at Malone was arguably the most impactful period of my life. I was completing research for my honors thesis and needed a place to stay during the summer to conduct my research. Marcia Everett, who I was privileged to work alongside as a Course Assistant for three years, opened her home free of charge, and her life free of reservation. In addition, I had many friends who sacrificed time and sleep to help me with my project and pray for me, even when I untruthfully declared that I was "fine." Every moment at which I felt weak, inadequate, unintelligent, incapable, tired, there was an army of community fighting for me and with me.

This community that I speak of, while a beautiful, humbling, and rewarding experience, also comes with pangs of disillusionment and unmet expectations. Such a community, one that is centered around Jesus Christ, requires a divine faithfulness. As Mike Terry, an amazing friend, leader, and advocate, stated, "a community of people that embraces the cross necessarily embraces a deep and paradoxical spiritual reality. This reality is that when difficult circumstances are met with a kind of sacrificial faithfulness, *true* community is realized."

As I reflect on my four years at Malone, I can say with confidence that I have seen God create beauty from ashes and give me a garment of praise for a spirit of heaviness. I have experienced the most radical reconstruction as I have surrendered my comfortable, complacent isolation for participation in the sacred body of Christ.

Malone has become a huge part of my family. It taught me character and humility and helped me deal with adversity and challenges. Plus, it offered all the fun experiences any college student could ask for. This university has shaped me into a very strong spiritual woman.

Corina Newsome, Class of 2015
Zoo and Wildlife Biology Major
Honors Program, GEN 100 Course Assistant

Library, which had long housed the offices and laboratory of the psychology faculty, opened up for occupancy when the Psychology Department moved to Founders Hall. The Honors Program settled into the vacant space, and students renamed the area "The Treehouse." The Treehouse provided a place to study, consult with the Honors director, relax in the Honors lounge, and plan for thesis projects and defenses. Honors students presented their findings at Malone's student research symposium, at regional and national conferences, before their defense committees, and, at public thesis presentations. A tiny sampling of honors theses, which are available digitally via the Cattell Library, yields titles such as "Mystery Lost: A Catechetical Theology of Worship for Today's Protestant Evangelicals" (Aaron Bunnell '13); "The Fungibility of Sin Taxes: An Economic Analysis of the Effect on our K-12 Public School System" (Michelle Hollinger '15); "How Information and Security Technologies Affect State Power" (Joshua Campbell '16); and "Nitric Oxide and TNF Production of Pro-Inflammatory iNOS Pathway in Activated Microphages from Rats with Inactivated Melonocortin Receptor Genes" (Caitlyn Ridenour '17). Remarkable research indeed.

In 2016, the Honors Program was modified in two ways to encourage more students to complete the program requirements. For the first time, honors students could earn a nineteen-credit-hour minor in Honors. Second, to enhance and enrich the Honors Program, its curriculum was revamped. Among several changes approved by the faculty: a reduction in the number of honors sections of General Education required, and enrollment in at least one intensive, interdisciplinary study of a selected topic not normally included in other courses. These seminars were fashioned similarly to an older honors seminar model and the "Faith in the World" template. During the first semester in which an honors seminar was offered, students enrolled "Food, Table, and Community." They explored the meaning and spiritual implications of food culture, considered how sharing a meal together strengthened community, and prepared meals collaboratively at Dr. Marcia Everett's home every week.

High-quality research was not limited to the Honors Program. The annual student research symposium, first held in 2009, provided a venue for any Malone student to present their academic and creative work. This fête of student achievement testified to the level of rigorous scholarship being conducted on campus. As Nathan Phinney, then a dean and now provost at Malone, remarked in 2011,

> The symposium gives students a chance to present independent work they've been able to do during the course of their career at Malone. Research is a way for students to engage deeply in a particular field of study that they actually care about. Much of the work students do in college is learning things other people have already discovered. Learning basic facts about the world.

But research gives students the opportunity to create new knowledge, to learn things about the world that no one else knows. That kind of experience generates real, deep, and profound learning.

With each passing year, a growing lineup of undergraduate and, later, graduate students presented original research, artistic and musical compositions, and other forms of creative work at the symposium. Originally held in the Brehme Conference Center, the event eventually moved to larger quarters in the East Campus building, formerly Temple Israel, to accommodate the expanding number of participants. Malone students often went on to present their research at student symposia associated with the Ohio Foundation of Independent Colleges, Conference on Faith and History, Sigma Zeta National Convention, and the Professional Writing Conference, among others.

To help attract even more high-achieving student-scholars to Malone University, the Admissions staff resurrected Scholars Day, which had lain dormant for a couple of years, in 2014 and added the new VISIO event in 2015. First held in 2004, Scholars Day annually drew scores of stellar high school seniors to campus. These academically-gifted students were interviewed by a panel of two to four faculty members, and each wrote an essay assessed by members of the English Department. Top finishers were awarded a renewable full-tuition Presidential Scholarship, and

all participants received at least a partial scholarship. VISIO recruited aspiring college students who demonstrated vision and leadership in their high school, church, and/or community. Each year, two VISIO participants were awarded a renewable full-tuition scholarship, and, like Scholars Day hopefuls, every attendee received a partial scholarship. These and other scholarship programs, as well as a variety of Admissions events, drew students to Malone who brought an abundance of academic, creative, leadership, and athletic talents to the university.

One of the most significant changes during the university era involved athletics. In July 2010, administrators commenced a three-year process to withdraw from the National Association of Intercollegiate Athletics (NAIA) and join the National Collegiate Athletic Association (NCAA) Division II. In 2013, Athletics Director Charlie Grimes enthused over Malone's official admission as an NCAA school: "Becoming a full status member of the NCAA is a milestone for all of us. We have made a pivotal decision for the improvement and enrichment of our campus athletic experience for not only our fine student-athletes, but also for the entire Canton community." President King was similarly effusive about the new opportunities for athletics: "The Malone community is delighted to receive this approval, an acknowledgment of the outstanding efforts and excellence of our athletics staff and coaches. First and foremost, it reflects our ongoing commitment to our student experience and our objective in athletics to deliver a 'Christ Centered, Athlete Focused, and Coach Driven' experience for our student athletes."

For decades, Malone University and its cross-town rival, Walsh University, were members of the same conference and had moved from one league to another concurrently. It was no different in 2010. So, Malone University partnered with Walsh University when making the transition from NAIA to NCAA, and both schools joined the Great

Lakes Intercollegiate Athletic Conference (GLIAC) in 2011. One of the fiercest NCAA Division II conferences in the nation, GLIAC was comprised of private institutions of higher learning from Ohio and predominantly state schools from Michigan. Although every Malone team held its own in the conference, the golf team brought home the very first GLIAC championship in any sport in 2013. That same year, Coach Ken Hyland's golfers became the very first team to appear at a NCAA Division II National Championship.

One of the downsides of a membership in GLIAC was the league's practice of scheduling games and meets on Sundays. Complying with GLIAC's scheduling schema represented a significant shift in Malone policy. In 1995, for example,

Malone Memories

I'll never forget the first day I arrived on campus. The first thing I wanted to do was transfer. Little did I know that I would meet lifetime friends. The atmosphere at Malone University is so contagious that no matter where you are from, it feels just like home. The university really represents Christ's Kingdom first, even through athletics. I really enjoyed playing football, and it was a dream come true to receive a scholarship and receive an education while playing football.

I also enjoyed going to Jubilee during Spring Semester. I think every Malone student should attend. It is a great getaway from all of your studies and revel in time with your peers in a Christian environment.

I was a part of a small nursing class. We made it through thick and thin together. Since we graduated in 2015, there have been reunions and cookouts almost every month. We will absolutely carry on that tradition forever.

One of my favorite Malone memories took place in the Barn. One day, just randomly, some of my teammates and I went to the Stewart Room around midnight. The room was open, so we cut on the microphones and speakers and had an impromptu karaoke night for about three hours. I barely even knew some of the people, but we are still friends to this day.

I had the wonderful opportunity and blessing of being elected as Homecoming King in 2014. I also had the privilege of being selected as one of two senior baccalaureate speakers for our graduation commencement. Malone opens the door for so many opportunities that it is hard to wrap your head around. I would not change the years of my college experience for anything.

Brandon Petty, Class of 2015
Nursing Major
Malone University Football, GEN 100 Course Assistant

The very first NCAA Division II All-American from Malone was Tina Oprean '14, a cross country runner, who earned the honor in 2013. By the end of the 2016–17 academic year, Malone athletes had earned NCAA All-American honors fourteen times. In 2017, Duke Taylor '17 became the first Malone athlete to win a national NCAA Division II title. A multiple All-American honoree, Taylor won the national championship in the discus throw. During the university's first year of competition in G-MAC, Malone athletes brought home a conference championship in women's basketball and men's indoor track and field. In March 2017, the women's basketball team appeared at a national tournament for the first time during the Malone University era and the fourth time overall.

the school's forensics team qualified for nationals, but Malone's policy at the time stated that students could not participate in competitive events on the Lord's Day. Since the forensics team's appearance was slated for a Sunday, Malone had to drop out of the competition. Thus, athletic events booked on Sundays presented a conundrum for the Pioneers. Fortunately, the situation was rectified in 2016 when Malone University moved from GLIAC to another NCAA Division II conference, the Great Midwest Athletic Conference (G-MAC). Formed in 2013, G-MAC was comprised of colleges and universities situated primarily in Ohio, but also in Kentucky, Michigan, Tennessee, and West Virginia. A preponderance of G-MAC members represented church-affiliated institutions, including Walsh University, which followed Malone to G-MAC in 2017. Given that most member schools were similarly Christian and that G-MAC did not schedule sporting events on Sunday, the new conference seemed to be a better fit for Malone University.

Malone athletes excelled in NCAA Division II competitions, whether in GLIAC or G-MAC, as they had done for fifty years in NAIA events.

Most athletes did not scrimp on academics either. Testifying to their abilities in the classroom, Malone students had earned fifteen NCAA Division II Academic All-American honors by the summer of 2017. The accolades were bountiful at the conference level too. Malone football and track and field star, Austin Cary '17, was named the 2016–17 Great Midwest Male Scholar-Athlete of the Year, and seventy athletes represented Malone on the 2016–17 Great Midwest Academic All-Conference Team.

In 2016, the Malone University Student-Athlete Advisory Committee began hosting an annual Malone Sports Awards event. Outstanding male and female athletes were recognized in the following categories: Top Rookie, Top Performer, Most Outstanding Team, Best Performance by an Individual or Team in a Game/Meet, and Breakout Performer. An annual service award was also presented to an assistant coach or other contributor to Malone sports programs. The evening culminated with the presentation of the most prestigious of honors, the Mr. Pioneer and Ms. Pioneer awards. The first to receive this award were Stephen Hunt '16 and Heather Papp '16. Mr. and Ms. Pioneer awards were given annually to accomplished athletes who best embodied the mission of Malone University athletics and the university.

Beyond the classroom or sporting venue, Malone students took on a variety of leadership responsibilities and enriched the life of the campus. As had their predecessors, Malone students during the university era mentored their peers as resident assistants or course assistants, served on Student Senate, performed in worship bands or with Chancel Players, led Bible studies,

competed on the Forensics team, contributed pieces to *The Aviso*, tutored their classmates, and captained their athletic teams. They found ways to serve their neighbors on campus, in Canton, and across the nation.

While it is impossible to catalog all of their service activities, a sampling here is representative of the whole. Nursing and pre-med majors volunteered at the Hartville Migrant Clinic every summer, education majors annually hosted a Campus Carnival for Exceptional Kids for children with differing abilities, the men's soccer team purchased school supplies for Canton Harbor High School students, and Zoo and Wildlife Biology majors embarked on a shark-tagging expedition with a team from the University of Miami's Shark Research and Conservation Lab. Malone students tutored area children at Lighthouse Ministries in southeast Canton, participated in local food and blood drives, and warmly welcomed refugee families to Northeast Ohio as they arrived from war-ravaged areas at Akron-Canton Regional Airport. Social work major Jenny Bushnell '18 shared her reason for greeting recent immigrants at the airport: "I wanted to welcome these refugees into our country because…they are often discriminated against. If there's anything I can do when working with refugees, it's showing them the love of Christ." In ways tangible and intangible, Malone students lived out the school's mission "to serve the church, community, and world."

Malone students were not confined to the Canton area or even the nation when serving with *and* learning about others. They traveled around the world and partnered with local Christian and other philanthropic organizations. As the university era opened, Celia King, long-time Director of Service-Learning, was still helping faculty, staff, and students prepare to serve with humility, grace, and hospitality as they ventured to Africa, Asia, Latin America, and Europe. In 2013, Ryan Donald was appointed as the first full-time director of service-learning and off-campus study opportunities in the school's history. As Director of the Center for Cross-Cultural Engagement, he built on Jack Harris and Celia King's exceptional foundation and facilitated service-learning trips to Austria, Denmark, Germany, Kenya, India, Israel, Poland, Thailand, Romania, Zimbabwe, and more. Director Donald also provided assistance to Malone students who chose to participate in off-campus programs. Malone students explored public policy and communications in the nation's capital, film-making in Los Angeles, music production in Nashville, or engaged in-depth study at Oxford University in England. Other students spent a semester in China, Jordan, Spain, Uganda, or New Zealand. Although relatively small in size, Malone University offered its students a rich and diverse selection of global study options.

The Malone community was likewise committed to fostering diversity and multicultural intelligence on campus. This was sometimes easier said than done. During the Streit era, Dr. Ken Stoltzfus and students from his Methods of Social Research class conducted a survey on campus about difference and ethnicity. They found that students of color were less likely to feel comfortable at Malone than the majority population. A concerted effort to attract more faculty, staff, and students of color and enhance the experience of international and minority students on campus was already in place, but the study demonstrated the importance of persistence. Brenda Stevens, Director of Multicultural Services, still had the herculean task of creating welcoming spaces for international students and native-born students of African, Asian, Latino, and Native American descent. Peer mentors, the Gospel Choir, workshops, film discussions, and guest speakers offered opportunities for conversation and assistance for multicultural students and their white classmates. International-themed events and heritage months, which commemorated the contributions of Black, Hispanic, Asian, and Pacific Island Americans, provided Malone students a plethora of ways to celebrate their own ethnic legacies and those of their peers.

By Fall Semester 2016, the school was beginning to more closely reflect the ethnic composition of the region and Ohio. Eighteen percent of Malone's student body and over twenty-five percent of its freshman cohort were comprised of students of color. Although only 7.6 percent of Malone's professors were ethnic minorities or internationals that year, this still marked an improvement in faculty diversity over years past.

Students of color were not alone in feeling isolated at times. LGBTQI students often felt marginalized too. This created some tension between those who held to a traditional Biblical understanding of sexuality and those who promoted a broader interpretation of Scripture. Malone policy did not change, and administrators held fast to the school's long-standing policies, but the campus did welcome thoughtful exchange when Soulforce, an advocacy organization for LGBTQI students enrolled at Christian institutions of higher learning, arrived on campus in 2010. In 2011, Samuel Taylor '13 founded Safe Space for LGBT+ students and their allies. Although not an officially-sanctioned club at Malone, Safe Space members secured the support of several faculty and staff, even some who were more conservatively-minded on issues of sexual identity, who opened their offices for any student in need of a safe harbor.

Although Safe Space fell dormant after Taylor graduated, the school was prompted to take up the issue more intentionally in 2015 in part due to possible modifications in government policies related to Title IX and a changed cultural milieu. In meetings with trustees, administrators, faculty, staff, and students, the university community endeavored to cleave to Scripture and still ensure a spirit of grace for all its constituent members. In 2017, the Malone community commenced a year-long conversation about LGBTQI matters with particular attention to their impact in relation to the institution, Malone students, and the Christian church. A task force, headed by English Professor Steve Jensen and Counseling Professor Christina Schnyders, conducted a series of forums, seminars, and campus-wide discussions on gender and

sexual identity. Dr. Jensen explained the purpose of the task force: "We will be exploring a variety of issues and perspectives as we seek to be faithful to Scripture, Christlike in our love and hospitality, and thoughtful in our response to a rapidly shifting cultural and political landscape."

Of course, it was important that all students felt a sense of belonging at Malone University, and campus leaders endeavored to make that happen. From the moment first-year and transfer students stepped on campus in late August, the community came alive with a variety of Orientation Week activities to help the "newbies" find their place at Malone. Upper-level students still offered a boisterous welcome to new freshmen as they arrived, although veteran students were no longer perched on the Alumni Gateway on 25th Street and instead shouted jubilant greetings from the new entryway on Cleveland Avenue. New Student Olympics—a Malone tradition—pitted College Experience sections against each other with prizes for the winning teams. Camp Gideon, Into the Streets, and the annual musical chairs competition remained staple traditions during Orientation Week.

Later in the academic year, Davenport Derby, Nike Air Band, and the Homecoming Dance, all well-entrenched rituals by the time President King arrived, and a host of other events offered students a rich campus life. A favorite was the annual Christmas Banquet. First held as a chili dinner in Osborne Hall in 1990, the annual affair progressed to a festive feast in the Dining Commons later that decade. This yearly Christmas gala gave students the chance to don their sartorial finery and savor the finest culinary delights AVI Fresh master chefs had to offer. Faculty and staff, adorned in elf or Santa hats, served as wait staff at the holiday event.

During the university era, Student Development also sponsored Chaos Day, Campus Block Party, Fall Harvest Party, Christmas Open House, Alternative Gift Market, Sock Wrestling, and World Issues Awareness Week. The event perhaps most illustrative of the Christian forms of merrymaking found at Malone was PGB's Root Beer Keg and Hog Roast.

Academic departments scheduled events for the campus community too. Election Parties, sponsored by Student Development and the Department of History, Philosophy and Social Sciences every four years, brought faculty and students together in the Stewart Room to watch the unfolding results of the quadrennial U.S. presidential race. Costume contests, trivia games, and razor-thin margins, such as those in 2000 and 2016, kept many students glued to their seats until the wee hours of the morning. The Department of Bible, Theology, and Ministry hosted a fall picnic for a time of food, fellowship, and worship for its majors. The School of Nursing and Health Sciences held an annual Pinning and Graduate Hooding ceremony at which the Rev. Dr. Linda Leon blessed the hands of each graduating nurse and Dean Debra Lee charged the graduates to "embrace their work as a calling, to pursue it with zeal and purpose." Several departments hosted year-end banquets for their majors, graduating seniors, and alumni. Malone University amusements and celebrations came in many forms.

The bonds of friendship forged at Malone did not end with graduation. The Malone Alumni Association found ways to engage graduates long after they received their diploma. The annual awards banquet functioned as the premier alumni

event, as it had since the Bible college years. However, it was not until 1962 that alumni were recognized by the college for their notable accomplishments. In 2002, the Young Alumnus/na of the Year, Graduate Programs Alumnus/na of the Year, and the Degree-Completion Program Leadership Excellence awards were added to a growing constellation of alumni honors. The new awards were established to acknowledge the contributions of non-traditional and younger alumni and the broader expanse of degrees and programs being offered at Malone since Dr. Spring was first honored in 1962.

In addition to the century-old Alumni Association, Malone University sponsored two other associations, the Malone Young Alumni Community Board of Directors and the Malone Multicultural Alumni Association. The Alumni

Malone Memories

It was the week after freshmen orientation at Malone University and the adrenaline on campus quickly turned into melatonin as the reality of a college education began to sink in. Not only were students struggling to adjust to the workload in college, they were also struggling to fit into their new social environment. I was one of these students. My friend group the first week of orientation slowly began to dissipate as relationships on sports teams and in residence halls began to grow and strengthen. For some odd reason, I wasn't able to quite gain my social footing the first few weeks of school and it began to weigh on me.

Luckily for me, the Malone community consists of people who look to include rather than exclude. My resident director at the time (who now happens to be a good friend of mine) took the time to come to my room and invite me to go line dancing with a large group of students and faculty members. I obliged and from that moment on I submerged myself into the Malone community. In some ways, I view that event as my "initiation" into the community at Malone, which is humorous because normally when one thinks of an initiation on a college campus they think of elite fraternities or sororities hazing and abusing members to see if they are "worthy" of being in their group of "brothers" or "sisters." At Malone, it is a different story. Instead of the high conditions that need to be met to make it into a group of people, there often is an *unconditional* seeking and acceptance of those who are on the fringes, of those who need a friend. I witnessed this kind of community at Malone over and over again.

Why is this the case at Malone? It is because the community is informed by a different reality; a Kingdom reality. The love of Christ unconditionally seeks us out and offers us an intimate relationship with our Father in Heaven. That truth and reality is at the core of the Malone community so that those who may be cast out by the standard of the world find a welcoming home on the corner of Cleveland Avenue and 25th street.

Interestingly enough, after I was accepted into the community unconditionally, I found myself doing the same to others on campus who found themselves on the outside looking in. By the grace of God and the example given to me by those before me at Malone, I was able to include and make others feel at home. Now, in a very real sense, Malone is home for myself and many others.

Mike Terry, Class of 2015
Bible and Theology Major
Honors Program, Student Senate President

Relations Office hosted an annual campus prayer walk, networking opportunities, career services, trips to local sports events, and excursions to destinations of cultural or historical significance. The expansion of alumni programs was largely due to Director Deborah Robinson. The longest-serving alumni director in the school's history, she brought her enthusiasm, organizational skills, and love of Malone to the position upon her arrival in 2000. As Director of Alumni and Parent Relations, Director Robinson also oversaw Homecoming and Family Weekend, published online alumni and parent newsletters, and founded a Parents Council to involve families more directly in the life of the university.

While the Office of Alumni and Parent Relations organized a myriad of events for Malone graduates, alumni often came together on their own. Perhaps the most renowned of all alumni gatherings was the annual Sloth game. Sloth may be one of the most unique, and oddest, sporting events ever invented. On October 31, 2002, Marc Fleagle '06, Michael Leggett '06, Kevin Pike '06, Matthew Repasky '07, and Ryan Walter '07 created a game that came to be known as Sloth. "Sloth" happened to be Matt's nickname, one of many sobriquets bestowed upon Malone students over the years. Sloth players made up rules and added to them with each competition. A "soccer-rugby-football kind of game," Sloth was played every Halloween and drew back alumni to the campus who in turn introduced new students to the game.

Over a decade after the original players started this Malone tradition, alumni established a scholarship for Sloth participants still enrolled at Malone University. Certainly, there was no lack of social frivolity on campus.

Of course, the spiritual wellbeing of Malone students remained an enduring priority during the King administration. Yet, the older "chapel service" model for worship was not especially spiritually refreshing or stimulating for a wide swath of students. After several years of study led by Rev. Leon, the chapel and Campus Ministries programs were revamped. Instead of fulfilling a required number of chapel credits, students were instead expected to attend at least twenty Spiritual Formation Opportunities (SFO) every semester. In addition to a traditional chapel service, renamed Community Worship, held every Wednesday, students were presented with a cornucopia of SFO options. Life Groups, smaller gatherings of students, were held throughout the day or in the evening. For example, be: Justice SFOs were held every Friday morning and not only fostered spiritual growth but also concern for the dispossessed. MU Bless Up, a weekly time of worship led by Malone alumni Cory Hunka '12 and James Talbert '13, was often a standing-room-only SFO affair. Between these and numerous Bible studies, Celebration, Worldview Forum, Woolman lectures, and Friday morning prayer meetings, students could choose from one hundred or more SFOs every semester. The Office of Spiritual Formation, formerly Campus Ministries, still sponsored trips to and offered scholarships, when possible, for the annual Coalition of Christian Outreach Jubilee Conference in Pittsburgh every February. Spiritual Formation staff members were dedicated to creating "a campus culture of Christian faith that encourages each student to grow in his/her relationship with God, develop a worldview rooted in scripture, and care for and about all mankind."

Throughout the university era, campus life at Malone University remained robust, the learning environment vigorous, and an institutional commitment to the mission steadfast. But preserving the Malone legacy meant that the university must actualize plans for a viable and dynamic future. After Malone was reaccredited for another ten years by the Higher Learning Commission (HLC) in 2013, members of the university began to craft a new and workable strategic plan. Although the college community had developed a strategic plan in 1998, it had never been fully implemented. In anticipation of the 125th anniversary of the founding of Malone and in keeping with HLC requirements, school officials implemented the new master plan in 2014. Entitled the Malone University Strategic Plan 125 & Beyond, the plan was a "blueprint to ensure a vibrant and transformative student learning experience while advancing" the university's mission, vision, and Foundational Principles beyond its first 125 years. Organized around the themes of Vibrancy (transforming students), Visibility (building the university's reputation) and Viability (improving financial margins), the plan was crafted and vetted by a committee of

administrators, faculty, and staff. In keeping with Malone's tradition of shared governance, community meetings were held in which employees prioritized strategic plan projects, offered suggestions for the future, and advised the administration on what was working and what was not.

With a flexible, but focused, strategic plan in place, the university was ready to commemorate its 125th anniversary with a flurry of activities. The celebratory year began on March 17, 2016. As always on St. Patrick's Day, students were treated to slices of birthday cake, and, for the first time, the Advancement team launched an annual "Day of Giving" fund drive. Shortly after the start of the 2016–17 academic year, a multimedia project, entitled "125 Voices," featured personal reflections and photographs from members of the Malone community and a commemorative video. The reflections and video were posted on the Malone web page and YouTube. The anniversary celebration was off to an auspicious start, and many more events were to follow.

In September 2016, nearly sixty participants cycled 125 kilometers or 12.5 miles in Pioneer 125: Ride for Scholarships. The purpose of Pioneer 125 was to observe the 125th anniversary of Malone, raise scholarship money for Malone

students, and promote bike riding as a healthy activity. Since cycling was one of President King's favorite diversions, the ride through the hills and valleys of Stark County and its environs was fitting. Homecoming/Family Weekend 2016 saw the return of four former presidents, class reunions, and family fun. The Homecoming Court was duly recognized during the Malone vs. Alderson-Broaddus football game on October 8, although there was a stand-in for the queen, senior Haley Kool '17. Haley, a California native, was at Cedarville University that afternoon, powering her way on a volleyball court for the Pioneers.

In March 2017, the university celebrated Walter and Emma Malone's monumental undertaking in several ways. On March 12, members of the Malone community traveled to Willoughby Hills Friends Church for a Sunday of celebration. Walter and Emma had long been members of the church and served as its co-pastors for eleven years. It was the perfect setting to observe 125 years of Christian higher education in both Cleveland and Canton. Dr. Jacalynn Stuckey was asked to deliver a message reflecting on key historical moments and God's faithfulness to Malone University over the years. Five days later, on March 17, students indulged yet again in birthday cake, remembered the faithfulness of the Malones during a time of worship, and live-streamed the anniversary festivities. On March 18, the school hosted a 125ᵗʰ Gala at the historic Onesta Hotel in

downtown Canton. Recounted Deborah Robinson, "We chose to host the gala in Canton as one way to thank the community for welcoming us so warmly in 1957." Coinciding with the diamond anniversary of Malone's move to Canton, the gala was one way in which the campus acknowledged Canton's key role in preserving the legacy of Walter and Emma Malone.

On May 6, Malone University honored its 125ᵗʰ graduating class during Commencement ceremonies at Faith Family Church in North Canton. Dr. King delivered the commencement address. Shortly before the end of the academic year, the president observed, "This has been an extraordinary year in the life of the university as we have come together as members of the Malone community to recognize and honor all that the institution has done in people's lives since 1892."

And, so, year of commemorative celebrations came to a close.

Except for one more item of historical significance. On May 13, 2017, the Malone University Board of Trustees officially recognized Emma Malone as co-president of the Christian Workers Training School for Bible Study and Practical Methods of Work, the original name of Malone University. The Board's decision was not only timely, but also historically accurate. In view of her role as co-principal of the Bible institute with her husband Walter and her exceptional administrative skills, Emma Malone essentially functioned as co-president of the school. Walter and Emma were fully partners, they both believed that women were called to leadership roles in the church, and they adhered to the traditional Quaker testimony on gender equality. The 125ᵗʰ celebration "provided an appropriate backdrop for making this official," President King remarked, "drawing much deserved attention to the many ways that Emma's contributions live on in the quality and character of Malone today." As Trustee David Rawson '62 rightly noted, "It's about time."

Thus, this story ends where it began: with J. Walter and Emma Brown Malone. It was their deep desire "to aid young men and women to become soul winners and effectual workers for Christ" that led to the founding of Malone University. If that was indeed their hope, then the promise of their little school was certainly fulfilled. Eight years after the founding of the institute, the school's catalog observed, "Divine guidance and the Divine blessing marked the work from the beginning." One hundred and twenty-five years later, Malone is still a place where men and women are nurtured to serve the church, community, and world. Its graduates are pastors and missionaries, educators and healthcare workers, business professionals and zoologists, lawyers and media specialists, artists and musicians. Although the scope of the curriculum and mission has changed over time, Malone University is still very much Walter and Emma Malone's school.

Acknowledgments

I was an eighth grader at Willowick Junior High School when my father, James H. Stuckey, broke the news that he had just been appointed to a tenure-track position as assistant professor of history at Malone College. The family was moving, he cheerfully announced, to Canton, Ohio. This was a significant milestone in my father's life that had long been in the making. Ever since his years as an undergraduate, my dad had felt divinely called to teach history at a Christian institution of higher learning. My family was attending Willoughby Hills Friends Church at the time, so a liberal arts college with Quaker roots seemed to be a good fit theologically for my Mennonite father. My parents were thrilled.

I was *not* happy. I loved my middle school life and worshiping at Willoughby Hills Friends Church where Walter and Emma Malone had co-pastored decades before. In protest, I was determined *not* to attend Malone College after I graduated from high school. I wanted to enroll at my father's alma mater. However, my dad asked me to give Malone a try for two years and, if then, I did not feel comfortable there, he would support my decision to transfer. Wise man, that Jim Stuckey. Ever gracious, he was never the type of father who would say, "I told you so!"

Not only did I receive an education at Malone that would serve me well, I became a part of a community that really does manifest love and concern for its members and the world beyond. I was mentored and challenged by professors who invested themselves in their students. That includes the most influential mentor and intellectual role model in my own life, Jim Stuckey. Some of the first classmates I met at Malone have remained among my dearest friends. Since arriving as a

professor in 1999, I have learned from and been blessed by extraordinarily gifted professors and scholars, administrators and staff. Really smart people who continue to pour into the lives of their students and colleagues, and who, fortunately for me, have become lifelong friends. More importantly, to borrow from Quaker parlance, the Inward Light of Christ shines brightly within them.

Of course, little did I imagine I would follow my dad's footsteps and begin teaching history at Malone the very same year he retired. I could not imagine laboring anywhere else. I love my work as an educator because of Malone's students. I could wax eloquent endlessly about them, but suffice it to say they continue to bring joy, energy, new perspectives, and delightful surprise into my life every day. Malone has been a good place for me to be.

Even so, when President David King first asked me to write a commemorative history of Malone University three years ago, I did not quite feel up to the task. How does one cover 125 years of history in one volume? One of my colleagues, Dr. Jay Case, rightly reminded me of my long history with Malone University and the lasting effect the university has had on my life and those of my loved ones.

It's true. Like me, all three of my siblings, Jodi '78, Jay '83, and Jon '86, are graduates of Malone. Other family members passed through its halls too: Mark Benedict '79, Shari Taylor-Stuckey '87, Shauna Welling Roberts '09, Ethan Baker '10, and daughter Jenaye '10. My mother, Janice Stuckey, immersed herself in the Malone community upon our family's arrival in 1969. She enrolled in classes at Malone, served as an advisor for Delta Theta Lambda, participated in Bible studies with Catherine DeVol Cattell and the Randalls, and was active in the now long-defunct Faculty Wives Club. Happily, my niece, Blake Stuckey '20, is studying at Malone University, and so the family tradition continues. We are all deeply grateful for the abundant blessings that have come from our association with Malone University.

Throughout the process of writing this book, I came to appreciate more fully the history and legacy of Emma and Walter Malone and their school. Within these pages, I have tried to include as much of the Malone narrative as I could in hopes that readers will find some personal connection with their own Malone stories. So, at times, this volume may read as if I included everything but the kitchen sink therein, but I hope an overarching narrative is evident. On the other hand, this was never intended to be an exhaustive history of Malone

University. A more rigorous and thoroughly academic treatment of the institution will have to wait for another day.

One of the themes that I hope has been apparent in the book is the importance of community at Malone University. This written tribute to my alma mater would never have come to fruition without my own inestimable community of family, friends, and colleagues. I am especially grateful to Diane Chambers, Malone University Professor of English Emerita, who served as the primary editor for this project. Not only did she read each chapter carefully and offer helpful commentary, but Diane was also my sounding board as I worked through the outline and content of the book. We spent countless hours in conversation at local eateries over this book, and we could probably offer recommendations for most restaurants in the Akron-Canton area.

Many of the wonderful "tidbits" incorporated into this book are courtesy of Autumn Berry Terry '15, who spent a summer in the archives as my research assistant combing through fifty years' worth of issues of the *Malone Messenger* and *The Aviso*. I also drew from Autumn's excellent undergraduate honors thesis, "The Historical Evolution of Malone: A Challenge to Keep Christ First in the Journey from Bible College to Christian Liberal Arts University," for my discussion of the "Malone Experiment." She is an exemplar of the type of graduate Malone sends forth every year at Commencement.

These two brilliant women were not the only Malone colleagues whose imprint is on this commemorative history. Professor of Theology Stephen Moroney, who has contributed in innumerable ways to the intellectual and spiritual vigor of the university, also read through the manuscript and offered insightful and useful comments. I am so very thankful for his assistance.

Previous histories about Malone written by President Byron L. Osborne and Professor John Oliver, my academic adviser while I was a student at Malone, were invaluable resources. The writings of Max Haines, my mother's cousin and *de facto* historian of Berne, Indiana, offered crucial insights on a rather obscure chapter in the school's history. As a result, I learned about the origins of the Light and Hope Orphanage in Berne, its move to the banks of the Vermillion River in northeast Ohio, and the decision of its founders to transfer operational control to Friends Bible Institute in 1911. Special thanks to Ezra Tkach '14 for taking me to view what remains of the orphanage, which happens to be located near his hometown.

Former and current members of the Department of History, Philosophy, and Social Sciences, participants in the Malone Writers Group, and other valued co-workers at Malone—among them, Becky Albertson, Amber Balash, David Beer, James Brownlee, Jay Case, Marcia Everett, Malcolm Gold, Shawn Floyd, Steve Jenson, Deborah Kwak, Greg Miller, Suzanne Nicholson, Terri Pearson, Matt Phelps, Allen Plug, Beth Rettew, Lauren Seifert, Donald Tucker, Scott Waalkes, and Dave Yakley—offered words of encouragement, counsel, and prayer as I worked my way through these pages. I am grateful to Malone's former provost, Don Tucker, and the current provost, Nate Phinney, for approving a research grant in 2015 and a course-load reduction during the 2015–16 academic year.

My deepest gratitude also goes to Director of Library Services Rebecca Fort, Archivist Amy Yuncker, the entire library staff, Director of Admissions Linda Hoffman, Director of Athletics Charlie Grimes, Sports Information Director Mike Leggett, and Erica McKinney and Judy Barkan, Coordinator and Assistant Coordinator of Constituent Information, for their much-needed assistance. Thankfully, our department's student assistants, Ashton Crooks '17 and Christina Stump '17, pitched in too. Had it not been for these and other Malone folks, the book would still be a work in progress.

Of course, all omissions and errors, historical and otherwise, are my own.

Historians love to read, and I am no exception. It is not unusual for me to participate in two or three book discussion groups during the summer months. Throughout the year, however, these amazing women, all Malone faculty or faculty wives—Elisa Case, Diane Chambers, Jennifer Estes, Marcia Everett, Tanya Hershberger, Darla Miller, and June Phelps—offer a sacred space for conversation and uplift during our monthly book club gatherings. They were a valued source of encouragement throughout the writing process and are equally delighted that this project is finally completed.

I am blessed with a treasure of family members and lifelong friends who knew me "back when" and

are much cherished. Needless to say, my mother, siblings, and extended family were unconditionally supportive during the course of this project. They are an exceptional bunch, and Malone University will always remain close to their hearts. Just as Malone was always near and dear to my late father, Jim Stuckey. Long-time friends Pam Mason King '77, Debbie McElroy Linton '77, Cheri Smith Ramsburg '80, and childhood friend, Marie Snyder Wargo, prayed for and bolstered me as I sometimes struggled through the research and writing. In the days and months after our forty-year class reunion in October 2017, Chris Dymale Cornillie '77, Debbie Van Fossen Hardesty '77, and Denise Moschell Stafford '77 offered extra

encouragement and prayer as I pressed to finish this volume. They all are a gift from Above.

The most remarkable people I have ever met in my life are my three adult children: Nicholas, Jenaye, and Lena. Generous of spirit and extraordinarily wise, they are pillars of strength, unceasing sources of inspiration, and steadfastly present. Although only one is a Malone graduate, all three are ever loyal to Malone and its mission.

As Malone University looks forward toward its next 125 years, may the Malone community be abundantly blessed and may it continually seek "Christ's Kingdom First."

Jacalynn J. Stuckey '77
Spring 2018

Appendix I

Malone University Mission, Foundational Principles, and Doctrinal Statement

Mission

The mission of Malone University is to provide students with an education based on biblical faith in order to develop men and women in intellectual maturity, wisdom, and Christian faith who are committed to serving the church, community, and world.

Foundational Principles

A Christian university for the arts, sciences, and professions, Malone grounds its educational mission in the biblical call to seek Christ's Kingdom First in all things. As we work out our calling, we put into action foundational principles that reflect our Christian faith, our Evangelical Friends heritage, and our desire to seek truth. These foundational principles help guide our work over time in the face of changing external exigencies and are the means by which we articulate what is and has been intrinsically important to the institution.

We cultivate the life of the mind by pursuing and witnessing to the Truth.

The academic life of Malone University falls under a broader goal of seeking truth in all areas, including the humanities, arts, sciences, social sciences, personal health, theology, and the professions. We value and foster intellectual breadth and virtue, believing that individuals who seek Christ's Kingdom First are called to embark on a lifelong process of learning. The quest for knowledge and truth enables us to be better stewards of God's creation. As people who are being transformed by Christ, we witness to the truth in many ways, such as engaging in research, scholarly inquiry, and professional endeavor; working for justice; and strengthening community life.

We are called to know Christ and make Him known through the integration of learning and faith.

We believe that faith and knowledge are inextricably bound to one another and should not be compartmentalized or fragmented. Professors and students at Malone examine what the Christian faith has to say about a given discipline and what that discipline has to say about the Christian faith. These actions stem from our belief that Christ is known not only through Scripture, the workings of the Holy Spirit, and tradition, but also through the pursuit of knowledge. We are called to make Christ known through scholarship in our individual disciplines, evangelism to our community, and service to others. These actions reflect our conviction that a Malone education should equip students to fulfill their callings. Therefore, we nurture intellectual curiosity, creativity, critical thinking, compassion, and spiritual growth.

We are shaped by and draw upon our Christian and institutional heritage.

Our educational mission is rooted in our understanding of the historic Christian faith. This broad Christian tradition provides us with a Christocentric perspective of intellectual inquiry and engagement with the world. Consistent with evangelicalism, the college has maintained its concern for biblical faith, proclamation of the gospel, and service to local and international communities. Shaped by our holiness and Friends heritage, Malone is an institution that values piety, concern for ordinary people, and experiential activism. From its founding, Malone University has welcomed staff members from different Christian denominations and traditions, enriching the resources of the university. The dialectics that emerge from these diverse perspectives compel us to an ongoing process of communication with one another and the community at large. This variety of Christian experience offers a basis for openness in the learning process, critical examination of worldviews, and cultivation of individual spiritual journeys.

Because we are called to love our students, we intentionally focus our work on promoting their intellectual, spiritual, and social growth.

The congenial and collegial atmosphere at Malone reflects a theological and intellectual commitment by the faculty, staff, and administration to educate and disciple our students in ways that challenge their intellect, encourage their faith and develop their character. We hold that learning flourishes in a community where people draw upon Scripture, tradition, reason, experience, and inquiry through thoughtful conversation and active relationships with others. The relationships that are formed between members of our campus community and students foster a dialogical process that reflects this belief that learning is not a solitary activity, designed for self-interested ends.

We live and learn in a community that manifests and develops concern for others.

As a university community we are called to learn from one another, develop relationships, and work out our vocations in ways that demonstrate concern, accountability, respect, and humility. We extend these principles to the larger community and the world as we examine and endeavor to promote justice, civic responsibility, peace, and reconciliation. Through outreach, evangelism, and service we desire to witness to the love and grace of Christ. We emphasize corporate worship, prayer, study of Scripture, and other spiritual activities to prepare ourselves for learning and service, as well as to nurture and strengthen the spiritual life of the community. God's grace is evident in our communal life as we seek to live out this calling in a broken world.

Doctrinal Statement

Malone particularly declares its faith in the following Christian beliefs:

- One God, eternally existent in three persons, Father, Son and Holy Spirit.
- The deity of Jesus Christ, in whose person are united the divine and human natures so that He is truly both God and man; His virgin birth, sinless life, miracles, vicarious and atoning death; His bodily resurrection and ascension to the right hand of the Father, and His personal return in power and glory.
- The present ministry of the Holy Spirit convincing sinners of sin and regenerating, sanctifying, guiding and empowering believers.
- The plenary inspiration of the Scriptures, their essential unity and their inviolable authority.
- The fall of man through the sin of our first parents; the death and hopelessness of man apart from the work of redemption wrought by Jesus Christ.
- Reconciliation with God through the sacrificial death of Jesus Christ by repentance for sin and receiving forgiveness and new life by faith in Jesus Christ as Savior.
- Sanctification of the reconciled believer through the operation of the Holy Spirit by the complete dedication of believers to God and the receiving by faith of cleansing from enmity against God; by walking in daily obedience as true and fervent disciples of our Lord Jesus Christ and growing more like Him in maturity of character; and by following the guidance of the Holy Spirit and receiving His empowerment for continuous victory over sin and service unto God.
- Our obligation to proclaim the gospel of Jesus Christ, making disciples of all men everywhere.
- The spiritual unity of all believers in our Lord Jesus Christ.
- The immortality of the soul, the resurrection of the body, the final judgment of the world by our Lord Jesus Christ, resulting in the eternal fellowship of the righteous with God, and the eternal separation of the wicked from God.

Appendix II

Documentation

All citations, sources, and references for this commemorative history can be found in the Malone University Archives:

Malone University Cattell Library
2600 Cleveland Avenue NW
Canton, OH 44714
330.471.8317

CPSIA information can be obtained
at www.ICGtesting.com
Printed in the USA
BVHW021644261118
534011BV00007B/225/P